AN UNREASONABLE ACT? FOR
Central-local government conflict and the Housing Act 1980

RAY FORREST
ALAN MURIE

S·A·U·S Study No.1

UNIVERSITY
OF·BRISTOL

SCHOOL·FOR·ADVANCED·URBAN·STUDIES

The School for Advanced Urban Studies was established jointly by the University of Bristol and the Department of the Environment in 1973 as a post-experience teaching and research centre in the field of urban policy. In addition to the dissemination of material in courses and seminars the School has established three publications series: **SAUS Studies, Occasional Papers and Working Papers.**

General enquiries about the School, its courses, research programme and publications may be addressed to the Publicity Secretary.

School for Advanced Urban Studies
Rodney Lodge
Grange Road
Clifton
Bristol BS8 4EA

Telephone: (0272) 741117

Director: Professor Murray Stewart

CONTENTS

ACKNOWLEDGEMENTS

We should like to thank all those who co-operated in this study: the officers and members of Norwich City Council who provided extensive documentation and a series of interviews; Robin Sharp at the Department of the Environment for his comments on the draft report; Peter Bolan at Bristol Polytechnic for his assistance and encouragement; Martin Loughlin at the London School of Economics for his interest and comment throughout. Michael Hill at SAUS and Peter Saunders at Sussex University also provided various insights incorporated in the final version.

The structure and style of the book and the conclusions drawn are, of course, the total responsibility of the authors.

The study was funded by the Government and Law Committee of the Economic and Social Research Council, Grant No.E0023 2034.

The following material contained in the report is Crown Copyright, and is reproduced by permission of the Controller of Her Majesty's Stationery Office:

> Section 23 of the Housing Act 1980, p 167.

> Notice of Intervention by the Secretary of State, 3 December 1981, p 169.

> Notice of Withdrawal of Notice of Intervention by Secretary of State, 7 May 1985, p 129.

> Notice in Eastern Daily Press "Tenants of Norwich City Council", p 92.

> Copy Department of Environment (Norwich) letterhead, p 115.

INTRODUCTION

On 3 December, 1981, Michael Heseltine, then Secretary of State for the Environment, announced in the House of Commons:

> "I have today sent a notice to Norwich City Council that I intend to use my powers under Section 23 of the Act to intervene to assist secure tenants of the council to exercise their right to buy their homes. I have taken this step with the greatest reluctance, and only after prolonged correspondence and discussions with the council over many months".[1]

In this statement he was referring to the Housing Act 1980 which had introduced a statutory right for the majority of council tenants to purchase their dwellings if they so wished. Section 23 of that Act contained powerful powers for central government intervention if, as was anticipated in the drafting of the legislation, any local authorities were slow or reluctant in implementing the Right to Buy.

Following the Secretary of State's notice of intervention, Norwich City Council applied to the Divisional Court for an injunction to stop him proceeding. The Divisional Court dismissed the application. Norwich City Council then appealed to the Court of Appeal and subsequently lost the action.

This study aims to document and comment on the events preceding the court action, the key issues and judgements in the legal proceedings and the implications of the outcome both for Norwich City Council itself and for the relationships between central and local government in general. In doing so, the report relates to a number of academic and policy debates.

There has been a vigorous debate in recent years around the notion of the local state, its autonomy and specificity. The perceived progressive centralisation of state power and the dilution and constraining of localised power has been a dominant theme in theoretical accounts of structural change in contemporary capitalism as well as among those more directly concerned with policy making processes and the role of local government in Britain in the pattern of allocation of resources. For example, Jones and Stewart have suggested that a Bill of Rights is needed to give constitutional protection to local government.[2] From a very different perspective, sociologists such as Castells have proposed that, "the great crisis of local government is the historical combination of three related but independent crises: the structural crisis of the pattern of capitalist accumulation prevailing since 1945; the crisis of the hegemony of the monopoly bourgeoisie; and the crisis of domination of the state apparatus in advanced capitalism".[3]

A series of events ostensibly concerned with a specific aspect of housing policy can thus be set within a much wider ranging debate. The circumstances of the intervention in Norwich are of intrinsic interest. It is a good story. It has a plot which twists and turns and, as in the best dramas, there is a court room confrontation between the main protagonists. And perhaps the outcome is what we would expect from contemporary fiction. It is not David but Goliath who wins. And it may be that David did not have a monopoly of wisdom and virtue and that Goliath was somewhat misunderstood. This report does not set out to pass a final judgement on who was right and who was wrong but to provide a relatively full factual account situated within an explanatory framework which appreciates the necessary but often contradictory relationship between different levels of government. It is in this way that the most abstract formulations such as Castells' are valuable in avoiding the tendency to ascribe anthropocentric motives to institutional conflicts - the vindictive centralist Secretary of State crushing the enlightened, localist council. There are, of course, real people making real decisions in this story and undoubtedly those individuals affect the contours of the conflict and the eventual outcomes. But the conflict represents more than a disagreement among a number of politicians and bureaucrats over the rate of disposal of a few hundred council houses. It represents more than a disagreement over the politics of housing policy. It is indicative of a particular structured tension between central and local government. To paraphrase the views of Duncan and Goodwin (among others), it is a representation of a social process, historically specific in space and time.[4] And to quote Castells, "The meaning of local governments within the whole social process of the state apparatus varies for each phase and stage of historical development".[5]

Having acknowledged the relevance of different levels of abstraction in the analysis this study does not have as its primary aim the elucidation and exploration of the various relevant theoretical debates. Much of this current theorising lacks any empirical referent, relies on broadbrush descriptions of central-local conflicts or well worn historical examples. In the chapters which follow our primary intention is to provide a corrective to this imbalance through a detailed account of the circumstances which led to central government intervention in Norwich over the issue of council house sales.

There are a number of issues of current political and policy interest which this study will address. To what extent can the Norwich case be seen as similar to other court actions involving central and local government? In what sense, if any, can they be seen as the product of similar strains and tensions? Is it valid to put Norwich City Council alongside the historical list of local opponents to central dictat (from Poplar to Clay Cross)? Or should Norwich be placed alongside an emergent group of radical local authorities such as the GLC and Sheffield as part of the broader political strategy of a new local socialism? What does the case tell us about the controversies over the role of the judiciary in political conflict? Are there significant constitutional issues involved and does this particular form of interaction signal a further erosion of local autonomy in the pattern of allocation of resources? Is it central rather than local government that has broken the established pattern and changed the rules of the game?

Inevitably these issues are highly political and controversial in nature, particularly given the general evidence of a sustained and penetrating attack on local government in Britain at the present time. The Norwich case may be seen as part of a general erosion of local government autonomy. But why was it Norwich City Council in 1981 and why was it about council house sales?

The two chapters which follow will address these issues by drawing on academic literature, political debates and policy documents. The bulk of the report will then concentrate on the case itself.

The evidence presented is derived from a number of sources. These include internal documents of Norwich City Council, transcripts of court proceedings, interviews with key local authority officers and members, Hansard and the local and national press.

In carrying out this study we set out with the intention of providing a full factual account of the conflict between the Department of the Environment and Norwich City Council. The distinctions between facts and nuances, biases and interpretations are, however, inevitably blurred. It would be hoped that a substantial part of this study is uncontentious in the sense that it is indisputable that certain events occurred and certain statements were made by certain individuals. The broader framework within which the story is set and the interpretations offered are, of course, open to debate. There is an implicit, if not explicit, sympathy with the role of local government and a concern with the perceived erosion of local autonomy and control. Nevertheless, the study did not set out to mount a spirited defence of Norwich City Council and a denunciation of the Department of the Environment. Neither are the conclusions couched in these terms.

But perhaps inevitably the story is told with a local government slant. It was the local authority which offered the research material in the form of detailed documentation of meetings and correspondence. Officers and members cooperated in lengthy interviews. Data and information were freely given without scrutiny or control of the final product. It would be difficult to imagine central government being similarly open about its decision-making processes. That is at least one reason for defending local government.

1
LOCAL GOVERNMENT, LOCAL AUTONOMY AND COUNCIL HOUSING

At one level the Norwich council house sales saga can be seen as a conflict over housing policy, as a political clash between a right wing central administration determined to sell council houses and a recalcitrant left wing local authority with rather less enthusiasm for the policy. Such conflicts between central and local government are neither limited to the issue of council house sales, to Norwich nor indeed to Britain[1] and whilst the current debates and conflicts are historically specific they are by no means historically idiosyncratic. The history of central-local government relations in Britain involves a continuous friction between central and local priorities and demands, between the legitimacy of local mandates and the policies of elected national governments, between local discretion and central guidance or dictat. Occasionally these tensions erupt, gain wider prominence and become symbols of deeper conflicts, variously defined as class struggles, opposition to authoritarian centralism, the erosion of local autonomy or the products of structural discrepancies in contemporary capitalism.

The dominant image is of the radical local administration resisting cuts, or wishing to increase expenditure on local services confronting a reactionary, insensitive central government. Such an image may be consistent with current events but presents only a partial account of central-local conflicts and is in danger of erecting party political differences as the key explanatory variable and local actions as the source of conflict. Inevitably the political complexion of the national government in power produces conflicts which appear to be party based and the progressive 'nationalisation' of local politics with increasing use and compatibility of political labels at national and local levels has highlighted this aspect.[2] There are, of course, instances where the political labels are reversed as in the case of the maintenance of selective schooling involving a confrontation between the Secretary of State for

Education and Science and the Metropolitan Borough of Tameside. Nevertheless, the most prominent conflicts have been between Conservative central governments and Labour controlled local governments. At its simplest level this is because at times of economic crisis it is expenditure on council housing, state education, the health services and other items of social consumption which are often hit hardest. Labour controlled local authorities are more likely to be resistant to those pressures and are more likely to have greater investment in those items. Historically, resistance to such pressures has resulted in legal action by central government to enforce the implementation of particular policies, legislation to control the expenditure patterns of local government more tightly or, indeed, to remove entirely the provision of a service from local political control. And this process has a long history. Whilst such conflicts have a particular prominence at the present time a tendency towards greater control by the centre can be observed since at least the 1930s.[3]

It would be misleading, however, to view central-local conflicts only in terms of those instances when the issue became the object of legal proceedings. Disagreements and conflicts over priorities are ever present. Moreover, centralism is by no means exclusively associated with Conservative administrations in Britain. Nor are local autonomy and democracy such unambiguously enlightened and progressive features. Indeed, enlightened local autonomy and dissension in one era can become reactionary obstruction in the next. Faced with a right wing central government local enclaves of socialist resistance have been heralded as the new terrain of class struggle - as prefigurative of a broader based socialist transformation.[4] But the rules of the game constantly change and conflicts and struggles find new institutional expression at different levels of the state at different times. In the 1960s and 1970s the radical left mounted a sustained critique of the role of local bureaucrats and elected members in the allocation of resources, and Cockburn's influential book characterised local government as local state, "a key part of the state in capitalist society",[5] primarily an instrument of class domination and control. Such an analysis has been correctly criticised as being crude and unidimensional, mainly because it involved an inappropriate transposition of theories of the central state to the local level. Nevertheless, some of those critiques have been rather easily forgotten with the general onslaught on local government services in recent years. And it is council housing which has been perhaps the area of greatest political and theoretical confusion. The rather timid campaign against council house sales by the Labour Party reflected a lack of clarity over what it was that was being defended. It reflected also a recognition of political realities. The mass mobilisation of tenants was unlikely. Put crudely, those tenants in the better council housing would want to buy, and those in the dump estates would not think it was worth defending. Indeed it <u>was</u> unclear what was being defended. It was certainly questionable whether an unqualified resistance to sales was a struggle for the working class or the preservation of local paternalistic, bureaucrat empires. In their discussion of the development of council housing in Sheffield Dickens and Goodwin comment:

> "Council housing, while it is under attack from a right wing central government, has at the same time, become a peculiarly repressive form of tenure. It has become far removed from the ideals of, for example, John Wheatley in the 1920s and Aneurin Bevan in the 1940s: ideals which were substantially upheld. But rather than continue glorifying past achievements, perhaps we should now ask: is council housing <u>as we know it</u> really something worth going to the wall for?"[6]

Despite some initial aggressive posturing few local authorities chose to go anywhere near the wall when the Right to Buy was introduced. It might be argued, however, that Norwich, the authority which came nearest to doing so, had council housing rather more worthy of defence than many others. If we accept this it might partly explain why Norwich was more likely to defend its council housing stock. It would not however explain why council housing in Norwich had developed in a particular way. To understand this we would need an historical account of the development of council housing and housing policy in Norwich. It is in this respect that some commentators have pointed out that concepts such as local state and an undifferentiated use of terms such as council housing are rather blunt instruments with which to comprehend relations of class, locality and broader processes of social and economic change.[7] It is these considerations and the limitations of a simple party political analysis which have led to a different debate around central-local government conflict and the nature and role of local government.

The essence of much of the recent academic work on local government is a concern with the theoretical distinction between the central and local levels of the state and the coherence of the notion of the local state. Following on from Cockburn's work a number of authors have attempted more sophisticated theorisations. Dear, in a paper entitled 'A theory of the local state', concluded by outlining eight key elements. The general theme was that the local state was strongly involved in the maintenance of ideological hegemony and in capital accumulation – that "local state form and function cannot be separated from those of the central state" although it did have a "distinctive spatial and functional constitution".[8] One of its key roles however was in facilitating "the locating of social pathologies at the level of the individual, family or community".[9] Thus the local state was seen to act as a kind of buffer insulating the key alliance at the centre between the state and capital from disruptive popular demands. Social problems, deprivation, the consequences of recession were thus localised and depoliticised.

Such a view related closely to a perceived duality of function between central and local government and a bifurcation in British political processes. Stated simply, it was argued that the state at local level was concerned with social consumption policies and open to pluralist influences whilst the key relations of production and policies of social investment were protected through a corporatist alliance between state and capital at the centre. Castells, for example, has described local government as the "channel of political expression which maximises the expression of the people's will within the limits of the system".[10] But interestingly, an element of the New Right critique of local government has been that the rights of individual citizens are not well represented. According to Bulpitt, the [Conservative] government objected to what it perceived to be an increasingly corporatist style 'carve up' of local affairs between councils and trade unions.[11] This corporatist alliance at the local level was pursuing a collectivist rather than an individualist ideology. And in Bulpitt's persuasive account of the territorial economy of Thatcherism he argues that "the major innovative feature of the early Thatcherite territorial code was its emphasis ....on the role of the ordinary citizen in the local political process".[12] The Local Government Planning and Land Act 1980, the Education Act 1980, the Transport Act 1980 and the Housing Act 1980 represented the legislative response to this view. The Housing Act opened up local housing provision to greater influence from private enterprise and the Right to Buy was a clear expression of individualism over collectivism.

The dual state thesis outlined above was a theoretical challenge both to Marxist formulations of the local state and the theorisation of central-local relations offered by contemporary political science.[13] The former saw local struggles as essentially class struggles whilst the latter described central-local relations in terms of negotiation and bargaining. For Saunders and Dunleavy local political struggles did not mobilise along class lines but according to differential access to social consumption.[14] Dunleavy called such groupings 'consumption sectors'.

In the political science literature there has been a continuing debate about whether the relations between central and local government are best characterised as a partnership or as a relationship in which local government is necessarily subordinate.[15] Work for the Central-Local Government Panel of SSRC used an inter-organisational theory perspective to focus attention upon the resources possessed by organisations which enabled them to bargain within a wider power context.[16] For Saunders, such perspectives missed the essence of the relations between central and local government:

> "....the dominance of central over local government agencies is best explained and analysed, not through organisational theory, but with reference to the dominance of investment over consumption, corporatism over democracy, and profit over need. In this way, the complexity of central-local relations can be analysed in the context of a broader appreciation of the state and political autonomy, thus combining the strengths and avoiding the weaknesses of contemporary political science and Marxist approaches".[17]

Such debates on the relative autonomy of the local state and its functional specificity merged progressively into a more broadly based concern with locality and sub-national social and economic processes. This occurred for a number of reasons. Firstly, analyses of the pattern of recession, unemployment, investment and disinvestment pointed to a spatial unevenness and distinctive local variations. This spawned an interest in locality based studies where the local state was only one concern among many.[18] Secondly, the functional distinctions between local and central state in terms of social consumption and social investment and the distinction between corporatism and pluralism seemed to break down under closer scrutiny. As Duncan and Goodwin argue:

> ".....there seems little historical argument for so rigid a separation between production and consumption. Much state activity, in the central concerns of law and social

control for instance, are clearly concerned with both. Similarly, housing policy, often the very stuff of urban 'politics' research, cannot just be designated as consumption. It is an important part of production in itself....."[19]

Thirdly, contemporary developments in terms of local political resistance to the Conservative government have also raised questions as to why that resistance should occur in some locations rather than others. It is inadequate to offer an analysis which is limited to local government and which takes no account of other local dimensions such as local class structures and patterns of employment which might explain the historical development of that localised recalcitrance. Castells, for example, has argued that local territories are the specific expression of the historical development of class relations. All local societies are, he suggests, conditioned by three sets of factors - relationships of production, relationships of distribution and culture.[20]

To understand local government, therefore, we have to understand the localities in which it is set. Concerns with local state institutions are now firmly enmeshed with studies of local labour markets and local culture. The focus of attention has therefore shifted from distinguishing central from peripheral forms and functions of state intervention to understanding the nature and significance of locality in all its dimensions. Local conflicts may not be seen directly as class struggles but the transformation of localities is seen as the localised expression of the uneven transformation of a class society.

In all these debates, council housing occupies a prominent position. Not only has its historical development represented a major and very visible ideological irritation for the Conservative Party but its management and allocation has been one of the major areas in which locally elected councils could exert influence on the local social and economic structure. With the extension of home ownership high on the political agenda (with its symbolic value as the extension of citizenship rights) the disposal of council houses has been in the forefront of a broader ideological crusade. These ideological considerations have, however, progressively taken second place to more pressing fiscal imperatives. Council housing, unlike the National Health Service, has always been a minority provision for the working classes. Moreover, unlike cuts in education and health, disinvestment in council housing has less immediate consequences. Representing, as it has, the soft underbelly of the welfare state, it has been caught in a pincer movement between an ideological commitment to individualism and the public expenditure imperatives of monetarism – an imperative which has increasingly fallen on local government expenditure given the failure of central government's macro economic strategies.

Much of what has happened to welfare expenditure in general and local government expenditure in particular runs contrary to the theoretical arguments of the early 1970s which saw the expansion of welfare provision, investment in social consumption,[21] or in the means of collective consumption,[22] as a contradictory but inherent tendency in contemporary capitalism. It was contradictory in the sense of extending a collectivist ideology within a system based on private property and contradictory in demanding ever higher levels of state expenditure when the source of state revenues was profit appropriated privately. This tension between state revenues and state expenditures was a fundamental structural contradiction which found concrete expression in urban fiscal crises which would ultimately lead to a serious rupture in the social relations of contemporary capitalism. It was argued that state expenditure was necessary to provide the general conditions for continued capital accumulation, for the reproduction of labour power and to ameliorate the social costs of the accumulation process (for example, unemployment and the uneven pattern of investment and disinvestment). A delicate balance existed between the growing tax burden for individual capitalist enterprises, the necessity of that tax revenue to enhance the general conditions for continued capital accumulation, and to maintain the stability of the system through expenditure on social consumption. The relationship between private profit and state expenditure was both symbiotic and contradictory. Any attempt to roll back the frontiers of the welfare state would lead to the imminent collapse of the system.

Recent events in Britain and elsewhere have, however, posed a serious theoretical challenge to this perspective. It may be that it is too early to judge the systemic consequences of the attempts to control and reorient state expenditure. But both theoretical and political debates have shifted and local government in Britain now occupies a prominent position in these. The squeeze on public expenditure has been disproportionately concentrated on those areas within the domain of local discretionary powers – particularly housing. Moreover, the rising public expenditure burden associated with unemployment has meant that in order to constrain the public sector borrowing requirement, rising central government expenditure must be balanced by reduction in local government expenditure.

Despite claims of profligacy and inefficiency at the local level it has been central rather than local government expenditure which has been less controllable. Attempts to reduce the overall level of public expenditure through greater control of local government spending have been more than compensated by the rising costs of unemployment benefits and the costs of policing the recession.

> "Put in crude terms,........the government's economic requirements - reduction in public expenditure - have been in conflict with the political impossibility of withdrawing state benefits from the unemployed (although there is a continuing attempt to chip away at benefit levels)".[23]

As a percentage of GDP public expenditure stood at 39% when the Conservatives came to power. After more than five years of determination to reduce that level it stands at around 43%.[24] It seems that a significant reduction can only be brought about by some drastic surgery on the welfare state. And the recent backtracking on reductions in student grants indicated the political consequences of cuts which hit the middle classes. Any more than minor tinkering with expenditure on education and health is liable to generate vociferous and articulate opposition.

An alternative method of reducing public expenditure and shrinking the size of the public sector has been the disposal of publicly owned assets. Perhaps because of the problems outlined above this has become a more prominent aspect of government policy. Between 1979 and 1982 £1,869 million was generated through the disposal of shares in state owned companies such as BP and Britoil and through the complete privatisation of companies such as Amersham and Ferranti.[25] Cash receipts from the sale of council houses since 1979 generated over £2 billion in the same period. Only the recent sale of British Telecom delivered a more significant amount but represents a one-off cash receipt. Receipts from council house sales now stand at over £12 billion and exceed the total from all other sales of assets since 1979. The sale of council houses has therefore been a major part of the government's economic, as opposed to housing, policy. Revenue from sales is now expected to decline over the next few years. For this reason we are liable to see new policies for the privatisation of council housing which depend less on the unpredictable behaviour of individual tenants. In retrospect the Right to Buy, far from representing the thick end of the wedge, may well be seen to have been the precursor to policies which effectively removed housing provision from local political control. If that happens local government will have been well and truly emasculated.

2

THE DEVELOPMENT AND IMPLEMENTATION OF GOVERNMENT POLICY

The origins of the Right to Buy

Policies and plans to assist and encourage council tenants to purchase their dwellings have existed as long as has council housing itself. The earliest housing legislation required local authorities to sell dwellings they built and inter-war legislation enabled local authorities to sell with Ministerial consent. The opposition to municipal ownership and support for owner occupation as the most desirable tenure form are constant themes in political debate both before and after 1945. They have been particular themes for Conservative party spokesmen. Accounts of the development of post war policies in relation to the sale of council housing would tend to identify the Conservatives leading a debate and developing their stance from enabling to encouraging and, finally, requiring sales while Labour lagged behind in developing their stance from prohibition to reluctant permission.[1]

In outlining the Conservative party's attitude to the sale of council houses in 1979 it is relevant to refer back to their last experience in government. A new Conservative government in 1970 had removed restrictions on the sale of council houses in line with their election Manifesto pledge to "encourage local authorities to sell council houses to those of their tenants who wish to buy them".[2] In pursuing their policy much of the earlier caution over both purchase prices and restrictions was put aside. Increasing reference was made to the 'Right to Buy' and decreasing reference to safeguards for the local authority. Some local authority representatives were demanding an increased discount for purchasers. At the 1971 Conservative Party Conference, the Minister for Housing and Construction announced his willingness for Birmingham as well as Manchester to sell at a 30% discount instead of 20% and stated: "I hope that others will follow suit". Commenting on allegations that in some cases, where Labour had gained control from Conservatives, councils were breaking faith with tenants by reversing sales policies the Minister replied that the electoral process was a better method of prevention than his interference with local government. However, he also stated: "I have a little list of Tory authorities which refuse to sell council houses",[3] and hoped that this list would be shorter in the next year. The whole tenor of debate had changed considerably from that of the 1950s and early 1960s. It was to change further with disappointment at progress with this and other housing policies after the initial interest of 1970-72 which included a growth in the number of council houses sold from under 7,000 in 1970 to nearly 46,000 in 1972. The decline from this peak after 1972 inevitably aroused comment within the Conservative Party.

At the Party Conference in 1972 it was urged that councils which refused to sell to their existing tenants must be compelled to do so, to sell at current prices, with an appropriate allowance for the years of tenancy and a restriction of, say, three or five years before resale was permitted. It was argued that this would still enable local authorities to pursue vigorously "that part of the housing need which is properly their responsibility - that is, concentration on slum clearance and housing of the elderly".[4]

At the Conservative Party Conference of 1972, the Secretary of State for the Environment claimed that the provisions of the new rent rebate scheme and the opportunity of purchasing homes at a 20% discount on the market price were greatly to the benefit of council tenants. He deplored:

> "those Tory councils which, from what I believe is normally bad advice of their officials, do not offer the prospect of owner-occupation to the tenants. I deplore also those Socialist councils which, out of political doctrine, wish to keep council house tenants as tenants and do not wish them to own their own houses".[5]

He went on to claim "we are beginning to succeed" and pointed to "good news" in figures which showed that in the first half of 1972 nine times as many council houses had been sold as in the same period of 1970. This, however, was "nowhere near enough" and Labour councils should be confronted with tenants "deploring the manner in which they have been deprived of this very basic right".[6]

If the number of council house sales was to be a measure of success in housing policy it was likely that consideration would be given to methods of boosting figures. The general consent was extended to Scotland and Departmental Circulars were increasingly admonitory. However, the general rise in house prices had taken the value of dwellings beyond a level which many remaining tenants wishing to buy could afford or were willing to pay. By 1973 the number of sales was falling in spite of government policy. No doubt this was partly attributable to the unwillingness of many local authorities to implement sales policies. However the fall in sales was also marked in new towns where there was no discretion in implementing policy and the tendency to see political obstruction as the principal factor could be disputed. Nevertheless criticism of recalcitrant 'oppositional' local authorities, both Labour and Conservative controlled, was increasingly regularly linked with suggestions that government should make it obligatory for local authorities to facilitate tenant purchase. By 1973 it was clear that any traditional reluctance to interfere with local autonomy, within either the Ministry or the Conservative Party, was wearing thin. The Party Conference was told that the sale of council houses with discount together with the Housing Finance Act could form a basis for election victory.

The Conservative Party election Manifesto of February 1974 included a commitment that, "subject to the right of appeal to the local authority on clearly specified grounds, we shall ensure that, in the future, established council tenants are able, as of right, to buy on reasonable terms the house or flat in which they live".

Although the Manifesto did not state on what grounds appeals would be made, it is clear that the intention was to limit the autonomy of local authorities. It was stated that the number of new home owners would have been still larger had certain councils not opposed the sale of council houses to those council tenants who were willing and able to buy them with the help offered by the government. Frustration, or concern at the failure to maintain sales at a high level, was apparently widely felt within the Conservative Party and merited a considerable change in the approach to local government. In the general election of October 1974 the Conservatives reiterated the promise of legislation to provide council tenants of three or more years' standing the right to buy at one-third less than market value, with a five year pre-emption clause.

The Labour governments of 1974-79 did not adopt the policy of a **Right to Buy** and amended rather than rescinded the general **consent** for council house sales. A circular amending the general comment was issued in 1979 and was designed to restrict the 'excesses' of some Conservative controlled authorities especially in respect of the sale of vacant dwellings.[7] The party political differences were as marked between local authorities as between governments. Labour's actions in government included elements which could be regarded as thwarting the locally elected authority.

The Conservatives in opposition between 1974 and 1979 had become more vociferous and determined exponents of a Right to Buy for council tenants. Their Manifesto for the general election in 1979 placed considerable emphasis on housing issues. The Manifesto referred to housing under the heading 'Helping the Family' and devoted one and a half pages to housing – more than to social security, or education, or health and welfare or the elderly and disabled. Helping people to become home owners was designed to support family life. At the same time the Manifesto's view that "unlike Labour, we want more people to have the security and satisfaction of owning property" was expressed in the context of creating a more prosperous country and giving more incentive.[8]

It is appropriate for this paper to quote the major Manifesto passages concerned with housing. Thus:

"HOMES OF OUR OWN

To most people ownership means first and foremost a home of their own.

Many find it difficult today to raise the deposit for a mortgage. Our tax cuts will help them. We shall encourage shared purchase schemes which will enable people to buy a house or flat on mortgage, on the basis initially of a part-payment which they complete later when their incomes are high enough. We should like in time to improve on existing legislation with a realistic grants scheme to assist first-time buyers of cheaper homes. As it costs about three times as much to subsidise a new council house as it does to give tax relief to a home buyer, there could well be a substantial saving to the tax and ratepayer.

The prospect of very high mortgage interest rates deters some people from buying their homes and the reality can cause acute difficulties to those who have done so. Mortgage rates have risen steeply because of the government's financial mismanagement. Our plans for cutting government spending and borrowing will lower them.

THE SALE OF COUNCIL HOUSES

Many families who live on council estates and in new towns would like to buy their own homes but either cannot afford to or are prevented by the local authority or the Labour government. The time has come to end these restrictions. In the first session of the next Parliament we shall therefore give council and new town tenants the legal right to buy their homes, while recognising the special circumstances of rural areas and sheltered housing for the elderly. Subject to safeguards over resale, the terms we propose would allow a discount on market values reflecting the fact that council tenants effectively have security of tenure. Our discounts will range from 33% after three years, rising with length of tenancy to a maximum of 50% after twenty years. We shall also ensure that 100% mortgages are available for the purchase of council and new town houses. We shall introduce a right for these tenants to obtain limited term options on their homes so that they know in advance the price at which they can buy, while they save the money to do so.

As far as possible, we will extend these rights to housing association tenants. At the very least, we shall give these associations the power to sell to their tenants.

Those council house tenants who do not wish to buy their homes will be given new rights and responsibilities under our Tenants' Charter".

The Conservative Manifesto referred in addition to "reviving the private rented sector" but it was the Right to Buy which formed the main plank in policy and to which the government attributed some of its electoral success. Mrs Thatcher argued:

"Thousands of people in council houses and new towns came out to support us for the first time because they wanted a chance to buy their own homes. We will give to every council tenant the right to purchase his own home at a substantial discount on the market price and with 100% mortgages for those who need them. This will be a giant stride towards making a reality of Anthony Eden's dream of a property-owning democracy. It will do something else - it will give to more of our people that freedom and mobility and that prospect of handing something on to their children and grandchildren which owner-occupation provides".[9]

When electoral success is partly attributed to the appeal of particular policies, and when the general inclination of the government is to repudiate consensus, to reduce the role of government and to encourage the private sector, Manifesto promises are important. The new government's decision to embark upon major new legislation immediately on entering office was encouraged by the financial background and economic policies which required substantial expenditure reductions and policy review as well as the policies developed in opposition.

The new Conservative government had revised the general consent on the sale of council houses to enable local authorities which chose to offer the more generous 'manifesto' terms of sale. But the major innovation in 1979 was the pursuit of legislative action to enforce the Right to Buy. Any hesitation about local autonomy, or housing need, or the terms of sales, had been overcome and the drafting of the Housing Act 1980 represented a determined attempt to ensure that neither the aspirations of those tenants wishing to buy nor those of Conservatives with respect to council house sales could be frustrated by local opposition or reluctance to act. The new mechanism to achieve privatisation in housing was Part I of Chapter 1 of the Housing Act 1980. This involved major changes in policy and practice towards council house sales. The principal elements and innovations in the new legislation were as follows:

1.   A statutory Right to Buy replacing local discretion and applying to the bulk of secure tenants with three years' tenancy and to all council properties (with the exception of some dwellings for the elderly or disabled and some other lesser categories).

2.   A statutory procedure for sale laid down to limit local variation over implementation of the Right to Buy.

3.   Very strong powers for the Secretary of State to intervene in local administration of the scheme.

4.   A price for sale to be determined on the basis of valuation less fixed rates of discount linked to the number of years of

tenancy (in any council or other relevant dwelling). The discounts were those introduced in the general consent of 1979 and rose from 33% (for three years' tenancy) by 1% for each additional year of tenancy up to a maximum of 50%. Procedures in relation to valuation, appeal against valuation, cost floors and maximum discounts are generally regarded to be very favourable to the potential purchaser rather than the landlord authority.

5. Discounts were to apply even where no pre-emption clause or other restriction existed. Save in designated rural areas (where a locality condition or pre-emption clause could be adopted) no preemption powers existed. The only disincentive to early resale related to repayment of discount (reduced by 20% of the total for every complete year of residence) if resale occurred within five years.

6. The legal right to a mortgage and the powers of the Secretary of State to determine procedures (for example multiples of income and age limits for mortgage qualification) to govern local implementation.

These and other details are generally regarded as providing very wide and detailed powers to the Secretary of State giving a capacity to influence local action and to maximise incentives to purchase. Since the implementation of the Act these powers have been consistently used in this way. Central monitoring and intervention have had significant implications for central-local relations. The Act does represent a thoroughly centralist, compulsory approach to policy implementation. Under the impact of this Act and the policies being pursued at the same time in relation to rents, subsidies, public expenditure and housing investment the nature and role of council housing is being changed and attitudes which have been associated with council housing since its inception are being significantly modified.

The powers to intervene

For this study and in relation to the conflict between Norwich City Council and the Secretary of State it is the latter's powers of intervention in local administration which are of particular interest. Section 23 of the Housing Act 1980 is reproduced as Appendix B in this report. In summary it states that where it appears to the Secretary of State that any tenants of a particular landlord are having difficulty in exercising the Right to Buy effectively and expeditiously, he may give notice in writing of intention to intervene. Where such a notice has been issued the Secretary of State may do whatever is needed or expedient to enable secure tenants to exercise the Right to Buy and the right to a mortgage. While the Secretary of State's intervention is in operation the landlord authority must provide documents and information and the Secretary of State receives any sums due to the landlord (as mortgagee), is not bound to account to the landlord for any interest accruing and is entitled to charge the landlord for any costs and recover these by withholding any sums due to be paid to the landlord. The intervention is withdrawn through a further written notice which could contain binding directions which could require the landlord to undertake steps different from those which the landlord would have been required to take if the Secretary of State had not used the powers of intervention. It is relevant at this stage to highlight two features of this clause. First, the basis for intervention is that tenants are experiencing delays and not a comparison between the performance of one authority and another. The Secretary of State is under no obligation to select the 'most dilatory' authority. Secondly, there are financial penalties involved in intervention - in respect of lost charges for costs incurred and interest on sums received on completion of sales.

This section of the Housing Act had not aroused enormous controversy during the passage of the legislation. During the second reading of the Housing Bill the Secretary of State, Michael Heseltine, had referred to it as follows:

> "Tenants wishing to become owners will expect the House to ensure that they have a right to buy which cannot be circumvented or ignored. If Parliament enacts this legislation it is right to expect all councils and landlords falling within the provisions of the Bill to carry out their duties responsibly and speedily. If it appears, however, that a council is not taking adequate steps to facilitate a sale under the Bill, I shall be able to take over the transaction. Clause 22 gives me the powers and discretion necessary to do so effectively.
>
> Let me say at once to the House that I regard that as a reserve power. I shall use it only when I find that I have to protect tenants from the illegal behaviour or deliberate delaying tactics of the councils under which they live - [Interruption]. As the hon. Member for Salford East (Mr Allaun) says from his sedentary position, it is democracy. We have a mandate to do precisely that".[10]

Other contributors to the debate made little reference to this section and financial and housing issues rather than local autonomy were mainly referred to in relation to the Right to Buy. Nevertheless reference to this clause was made by speakers from different parties. David Ennals, the Labour member for Norwich North commented:

"The right hon. Gentleman accepted that this was democracy. Is there not such a thing as local democracy? Is the right hon. Gentleman aware that in my constituency at the last election the local electorate had put before them by our Labour councillors the intention to do the exact opposite to that which the right hon. Gentleman proposes? Those Labour councillors received a bigger and better vote and won more seats than ever before. For them, that was as much a mandate as the one held by the right hon. Gentleman's Government".[11]

David Alton, the Liberal member for Liverpool, Edge Hill, stated:

"The Bill implicitly accepts that there are differences from area to area by deliberately excluding areas of natural beauty. Not only is it a case of one man's meat being another man's poison; it undermines the whole system of British local government and further erodes the right of locally elected representatives to make decisions on issues affecting their locality....

The Secretary of State argues that his policy is based on a mandate from the people. Some might argue that that is a strange mandate, as it is based on 30% of the popular vote. We also argue that every local councillor in the United Kingdom was elected on a mandate and that those councillors are also answerable to the electors who put them there. They, too, fought on policies and principles and they can be expected to rebel against what they will see as an imposition upon them. Unnecessary confrontation will be caused. The Secretary of State and the Minister would do well to listen to the exhortations of the Association of County Councils - which is controlled by the Conservatives - and of the Association of Metropolitan Authorities which have both condemned the Bill because it seeks to control local authorities".[12]

And Hugh Benyon, the Conservative member for Buckingham stated:

> "Many of my hon. Friends believe that the importance of the property-owning democracy overrides everything else. It is important and should be encouraged in as many ways as possible, but it cannot be the only objective.
>
> I did not join the Conservative Party to be centralist and autocratic, and I am in good company. In November last year the Chief Secretary to the Treasury had a great success in this House and that prompted the Daily Express to interview him under the title of
>
> "the Ghengis Khan of public spending".
>
> The article quotes him as follows:
>
> "You see, I have this deep instinctive belief that the more decision-making is dispersed throughout society, the less likely you are to get decisions with baleful consequences.
>
> Once you centralise power, a bad decision is disastrous".
>
> I could not agree more with that. It is all very well making the Secretary of State the gauleiter of housing, but on these Benches we should remember that the next gauleiter could be a commissar.....
>
> As a result of what we are doing this evening, attention and effort will be diverted once again to a totally barren controversy that will not produce one extra home. In addition, it will weaken and anger local government in the country. It will dog our footsteps in government, and if, God forbid, we ever find ourselves in opposition, it will be a precedent that will be used mercilessly against us".[13]

Inevitably there was a more direct discussion of this clause in the Standing Committee on the Housing Bill. Gerald Kaufman for the Labour Opposition referred to the clause providing the power for the Secretary of State to intervene as, apart from Clause 1 (which lays down the basic elements of the Right to Buy),

> "the most objectionable part of the Bill. Some of the clauses bestow upon the Secretary of State powers which are little short of dictatorial....."[14]

He continued:

> "Subsection(1) bestows upon the Secretary of State dictatorial powers which are not only objectionable to all hon. Members but simply do not fit in with the kind of approach which was foreshadowed in the Conservative Party Manifesto. It contained a section headed "The Supremacy of Parliament" which stated:

> "We will see that Parliament and no other body stands at the centre of the nation's life and decisions, and we will seek to make it effective in its job of controlling the executive".

> This clause gives executive powers without the power of Parliament to control them in any way....."[15]

The opposition placed considerable emphasis on the process of serving a notice under this clause and referred to the rights of councils and councillors to make representations and to delay the implementation of the Bill provided they could find legal avenues in which to do so.[16]

John Stanley, the Minister for Housing and Construction replied that:

> ".....what is at issue are the legal rights that are being conferred by Parliament on 6 million council tenants up and down the country. The only rationale and case for the clause is to ensure that those given rights in law by Parliament are in a position to exercise those rights, and that those rights are not merely paper rights but rights that it is possible to exercise in practice".[17]

He continued:

> "The Government's wish and hope is that the provisions of the clause will never be used. As my right hon. Friend said on Second Reading, we regard the clause as a reserve power. I suggest that among responsible politicians, whatever their political party, there will be a major failing of responsibility if there should ever be a time when the powers in clause 22 are used.

> I recognise that Opposition Members feel strongly and sincerely in their opposition to the right to buy. We feel equally strongly and sincerely in favour of the right

to buy. Having acknowledged that difference, it is quite unarguable that by the time the legislation has been enacted it will have passed both the national electoral test and the parliamentary test as a particular policy which has been stated in the most crystal clear and unequivocal terms over a long period.

Against that background, I suggest that there would be no justification, excuse or pretext whatever for people thereafter to seek to deny the rights that are conferred under the legislation".[18]

When challenged over the refusal of a number of Conservative local authorities to implement the Labour government's policy on comprehensive schooling John Stanley stressed the differences in the legislation involved:

"The Education Bill that the previous Administration chose to put forward did not specify that by a certain date there had to be comprehensive education throughout the country. It conferred a measure of discretion. If the hon. Gentleman is now complaining about the way in which his legislation was formed, that is his problem. This legislation is quite different. It confers a clear right to buy, exercisable from the time that the Bill is enacted, for those tenants who wish to use it. That is the nature of the legislation. It is an element of the legislation that we have put unequivocally through the whole process of the parliamentary proceedings".[19]

Stanley clarified aspects of the default clause as follows:

"There is nothing new in providing in legislation powers for Ministers to take over the statutory duties of local authorities where those local authorities are failing to discharge their duties. There have been successive Acts passed by both Labour and Conservative Governments in which reserve powers have been enshrined for Ministers to take over a certain function, or discharge a certain duty, where the local authority is failing to do so.

There are such powers in the previous Government's National Health Service Act 1977. There are such powers in the Control of Pollution Act 1974. They are

25

in the Education Act 1944, and in many others. The principle of clause 22 that there should be a reserve capacity for Ministers to discharge them is something that has been fully accepted by previous Governments".[20]

and:

"The extent to which these powers are used will depend entirely on the attitude taken towards the right-to-buy legislation when it is enacted. I have made clear already to the Committee that it would be the Government's hope and expectation that there will never be an occasion when the clause 22 powers will be used. We hope very much that local and national politicians of all politicial persuasions will take the view that once a policy has been enshrined in legislation, it is encumbent on responsible people in politics, whether at national or local level, to see that people are not denied rights conferred on them by legislation".[21]

He stated that:

"the process of buying a house and the process of taking out a mortgage in connection with a house is complex and technical. If someone was not a willing seller but was actually an unwilling seller who wished to obstruct the purchase going through, there are no doubt dozens, if not scores, of places where it is possible to obstruct the transaction.

It is impossible to provide in legislation for every single possible detailed circumstance where a particular purchase could be obstructed. The powers of the Secretary of State, if they are to be meaningful in conferring the right to buy where there is an unwilling seller, must be wide".[22]

When asked to clarify how the government would distinguish, on the basis of letters of complaint, between local authorities intentionally delaying and those where delays were due to legitimate administrative problems and shortages of staff, John Stanley stated:

"The first process obviously is that people will wish to write to Members of Parliament and directly to the

Department complaining about a delay. It will then be incumbent on the Department, in investigating complaints brought to them by Members of Parliament about delay or those that come direct, to establish from the local authority the reasons for the delay. That is self-evident. Maybe, in many cases - I hope in all cases - there will be perfectly good explanations.....There may be particular problems about defining sewerage arrangements and so on.

I can assure the Committee that within the Department, through our close contacts with local authorities and the experience of our officials, if a major local authority, or, indeed, a minor local authority, has given an instruction to try to hold up sales for whatever reason or is not implementing the legislation, the identity of that authority will be known very quickly. I hope there will not be any. Equally, it will be clear if the reason for the delay, in a particular circumstance, is simply that the local authority is doing its best but faces administrative and practical problems. I am certain that it will be clear which of those two situations arise.

All through this process, it is self-evident that Members of Parliament will be involved and that the media, no doubt, will take an interest in what happens. If it became apparent that the Secretary of State was contemplating serving a notice on an individual local authority, it is evident that the local authority itself would be aware of this. The Department would be responding to the local authority. It would be expressing doubt about the explanations given by a particular local authority. I would have thought that, over a period, possibly, of some weeks, or months, the local authority and the Department would have had a dialogue and the local authority would have every opportunity, before notice is served, to be able to indicate if it felt that the Secretary of State was behaving unreasonably".[23]

A question was asked about whether in every case where the use of these powers is contemplated, the Secretary of State will formally and in writing inform the local authority and give it the opportunity to make representations. John Stanley replied:

"As the legislation is drafted, there is no such precise requirement. But I am totally satisfied that if the Secretary of State was dissatisfied with the way a particular local authority was conducting itself and it was his view that the authority was trying to obstruct the right to buy, I have no doubt that the authority would be aware that the explanations it was providing had failed to satisfy the Secretary of State. The local authority knows the legislation every bit as well as the Secretary of State. The officers would no doubt be advising the councillors of the implications. I am quite certain that those councillors would be using every possible opportunity, if they felt that the Secretary of State was likely to behave unreasonably, to make their views known.

Taking Council X, rather than mentioning any particular one, I am absolutely confident that if the constituency Member for that particular council felt that the Secretary of State was likely to behave in an unreasonable way towards the authority, that hon. Member would be the first person to table parliamentary questions, adjournment debates and so on. I can assure the Committee that if there is any provision of this Bill which is most likely to be subjected to detailed parliamentary scrutiny and exposure, it is clause 22".[24]

The government did not consider it necessary to introduce a further statutory procedure to provide a formal opportunity to make representations. In view of the substantial and complex process which would vary from authority to authority and house to house the Minister also expressed the view that it was not possible to prescribe for this variety in legislation and that an element of willing spirit would be required in legislation.[25]

The debate in Standing Committee moved on to how financial and other arrangements would operate in the event of the Secretary of State having intervened. The Minister's concluding commendation of the clause as a whole referred to the equivocal position of the Labour Party which had failed to make it clear whether the legislation should be implemented or whether the Right to Buy should be denied to many tenants.[26]

The debate in Committee on later parts of the Housing Bill was foreshortened following a guillotine motion (16 April 1980). The discussion of this motion made little reference to the default powers in the Bill although the Right to Buy was widely referred to. David Alton, the Liberal member for Liverpool Edge Hill again referred to the mandates of local councillors and to the appropriateness of decisions on council house sales being made in the light of local circumstances.[27] The government's reasons for introducing a guillotine included concern that the opportunity to buy their houses should not be further delayed for those 'unfortunate' council tenants in predominantly Labour-controlled areas where the councils were still refusing to sell.[28]

Clause 22 was the subject of a government amendment during further examination in the House of Commons in May but did not arouse debate or a division.[29] In the House of Lords and the final reading of the Bill in the Commons the main attention in relation to the Right to Buy was focused on extending the categories of excluded properties (especially elderly persons' dwellings). It was over this issue that the government apparently conceded rather than delay passage of the Bill.

In view of the subsequent use of Clause 22 the relative lack of attention and controversy surrounding it during the legislative process is surprising. However, it is relevant to note that default powers in housing legislation had rarely been used in the past. Even the Clay Cross episode had not involved housing powers.

It may also be that some opinion was that action under this section would be slow and difficult. For example, the barrister Andrew Arden in his guide to the Act published rapidly after the legislation states that because of the financial consequences of intervention the Secretary of State would have "to comply with the requirements of natural justice, or at least of fair administration, before exercising these powers".[30] He expressed the view that the 72 hours between despatch of notice to intervene and enforcement is insufficient to comply with such requirements and that the local authority "must be given an opportunity to know and to comment on the Secretary of State's reasons or basis for action, before service of the 72 hour notice". Arden also considered the words "effectively and expeditiously" to have a degree of obscurity. He argued that comparison could not be made with a private conveyance. The demands on a local authority were different from those on solicitors "and it can hardly have been intended that at a time of staff reductions in the name of public spending cuts all authorities and housing associations should take on extra staff - and, especially, extra legal staff - to cope with these difficulties. It would seem that something more than bureaucratic delay must be shown to exist before these powers can be used: perhaps as much as actual wilful obstruction, or a declared intention to obstruct".[31] This view, while it may have been the widely held expert view, will be shown later to have been an underestimation of the scope of these powers and a misinterpretation of their nature.

Implementation of the Right to Buy

The sections of the Housing Act 1980 providing the Right to Buy came into operation on 3 October, 1980 - less than two months after its final parliamentary stages. The printed version of the Act was not available until very shortly before the commencement date. Although local authorities knew the broad outline of the legislation some detailed amendments - including those governing the sale of dwellings built for the elderly - were not clear to all those with responsibility for implementation until after the Act was available in printed form.

Central government from the outset took an active part in implementing the Right to Buy. The political and financial importance of this legislation meant that the task was not completed with the passage of legislation. The expectation of local obstruction, the desire to appeal over the heads of local administrations, and the desire to publicise the Right to Buy involved the central department with a substantial continuing role. Initially the government appears to have been satisfied to concentrate on publicity. In the financial year 1980-81 £530,000 was spent on advertisements on television and in national newspapers telling public sector tenants of their new rights under Part 1 of the Housing Act 1980 (including the Tenant's Charter and the Right to Buy). A further £125,000 was spent later in the same financial year on newspaper advertisements to remind tenants of the need to serve Right to Buy claim forms by 5 April in order to qualify for an 8 August valuation. In the financial year 1981-82, £239,000 was spent on publicising the Right to Buy. Information given in response to a parliamentary answer in May 1985 showed that the £2.3 million spent on publicity to promote council house sales was the largest campaign since 1979.[32]

In this same initial period considerable press coverage was given to local housing authorities which expressed an intention not to implement the Act. Most prominent among these were Greenwich and Rochdale. Rochdale were reported to have written to the Secretary of State inviting him to send in a commissioner to effect Right to Buy sales at no cost to the council.[33] At this stage Norwich City Council rejected a proposal that they should refuse to implement the Act. The Minister of Housing was at the same time making it clear that the government would use its powers. He was reported as saying these powers would be used "to ensure that tenants in Labour-controlled areas were not denied the right to buy".[34]

Although the Department of Environment has not been concerned to monitor the Right to Buy in terms of social or financial impact it has from the outset included progress in this area in the statistical returns made to it by local authorities. In addition the Department has obtained impressions on progress or delay through letters of complaint from or on behalf of tenants, from press reports or from informal discussions between the Department and the authorities. Where the Secretary of State received information suggesting that significant delays were occurring or likely to occur he normally made a formal approach on the question of current and future progress. In such formal approaches the Secretary of State usually sought overall statistical information on the number of Right to Buy applications received, the numbers at various stages in the sales process, and estimates of future progress. Where the information given in reply to such approaches has indicated to the Secretary of State the possibility that tenants have or may have difficulty in exercising the Right to Buy effectively and expeditiously further information and assurances have been sought. In typical cases this has involved meetings between the central Department and the local authority. Following such further correspondence or meetings the Secretary of State has either: stated that he will take no further action in the light of assurances, undertakings or indications of future progress (but usually requiring monthly progress statistics); or, where satisfactory assurances have not been forthcoming, given a formal warning that he is contemplating using his powers of intervention under Section 23 and requesting, within a specified time, further information on future progress. Where such a formal warning is given and the information supplied still appeared unsatisfactory local councillors were invited to a meeting with a Minister. After that stage the formal warning may be withdrawn but monthly progress information is still required.

This formal scrutiny and pressure was widely used. Indeed in

December 1983 the government was "in contact with about 200 local authorities, most of which are Labour-controlled, about aspects of their performance in implementing the right to buy". In January 1984, 176 councils were still subject to scrutiny. This represented a much more active and interventionist stance than had generally applied in the housing area in the past.

The first authority to receive a formal approach about progress was Greenwich. This was in November 1980 only some five weeks after commencement of the Right to Buy. As Table 1 indicates, a further three authorities were formally approached in January 1981, 11 in February, and 12 in March. By the time Norwich joined the list, 33 local authorities had already received a similar approach.

When Norwich's application for judicial review was heard reference was made to 70 authorities which had been approached formally about their progress with Right to Buy claims. Some 22 of these had made satisfactory undertakings (or in one case provided satisfactory information on progress) and no further action was contemplated by the Secretary of State. In a further 15 (mostly recent) cases correspondence and discussions were continuing. A further 23 authorities which had not initially made satisfactory undertakings had subsequently done so and the formal warning had been withdrawn.

The Secretary of State's intervention was clearly determined by other considerations and not by comparisons between authorities. Nevertheless the number of cases authorities have had to process and other comparisons were considered. The crucial measure of progress was the issue of Section 10 notices. These notices stating the landlord's view of valuation, discount entitlement, price and provisions in the conveyance and informing the applicant of the right to a mortgage and right to have the house valued by the District Valuer were to be issued "as soon as practicable" once the Right to Buy had been established. In addition to the rate of issue of Section 10 notices the Secretary of State considered the absolute number of admitted Right to Buy claims, the authority's housing stock and the relationship between these two figures.

The reason for focusing attention on the issue of Section 10 notices was that this was the last formal step wholly within the authority's control and not dependent on the response of the tenant or his solicitor. The proposed price and the draft terms and conditions to be included in the conveyance or grant are also vital pieces of

Table 1 : Authorities subject to formal approaches from the Secretary of State over the Right to Buy

Local authority	Date of 1st formal approach	Timetable subsequently agreed without formal warning	Formal warning issued	
			Subsequently withdrawn	Still in force at Oct '81
Greenwich	12.11.80			X
Barking	27. 1.81		X	
Sheffield	30. 1.81		X	
Sunderland	30. 1.81		X	
Doncaster	5. 2.81		X	
Stoke on Trent	10. 2.81		X	
Wolverhampton	10. 2.81		X	
Bolsover	10. 2.81	X		
Leeds	11.2.81			X
Camden	16. 2.81		X	
Great Yarmouth	23. 2.81		X	
Kingston upon Hull	23. 2.81		X	
Bristol	24. 2.81		X	
Manchester	25. 2.81	X		
Newham	26. 2.81			X
Lambeth	4. 3.81			X
Middlesbrough	6. 3.81		X	
Barnsley	27. 3.81		X	
Wakefield	27. 3.81		X	
Crawley	30. 3.81		X	
Leicester	30. 3.81		X	
Carlisle	30. 3.81	X		
Thamesdown	30. 3.81	X		
Hackney	31. 3.81			X
Lewisham	31. 3.81		X	
Walsall	31. 3.81		X	
Waltham Forest	31. 3.81		X	
Gateshead	15. 4.81			X
Haringey	15. 4.81		X	
Blyth Valley	15. 4.81	X		
Newcastle upon Tyne	15. 4.81	X		
North Tyneside	18. 4.81	X		
Birmingham	29. 4.81			X
Burnley	30. 4.81		X	
Norwich	30. 4.81			X
Tower Hamlets	30. 4.81			X
Brent	30. 4.81	X		
St. Helens	30. 4.81	X		

Source: Derived from Department of Environment Evidence at the Divisional Court 17.12.81.

information for the tenant in deciding whether to proceed with purchase. While these are reasonable justifications a case could be made for, say, focusing on the rate of processing acceptances, or the rate of completion. There are other stages where the local authority can delay or obstruct. An authority could issue Section 10 notices but with valuations or other elements which may require a second attempt. Authorities may delay the process of issuing acceptances or delay mortgage provision or completion by various procedures. The focus on Section 10 notices is not the only reasonable focus and is likely to produce a different list of 'offenders' than some other focus.

However, even if it is Section 10 notices alone which are considered there are a number of different comparisons possible:

1. At the end of October 1981 five of the 70 authorities being scrutinised had issued a smaller absolute number of Section 10 notices than Norwich. These were Tower Hamlets, Islington, Copeland, Chester-le-Street and Watford. The last two of these had made satisfactory undertakings. Islington had previously offered a satisfactory timetable but had indicated that they were unable to meet it.

2. In addition to these five authorities four others with whom progress had been taken up had performed worse or no better than Norwich when the number of Section 10 notices issued was expressed as a percentage of admitted claims rather than an absolute number.

3. When comparison is made in terms of statements about future progress Norwich's was worse than any other. Norwich indicated a date of June 1982 to complete all but 101 'difficult' cases. The only comparable case to this was Greenwich with 1,200 notices by December 1981 and a total of 2,165 by June/July 1982 - possibly excluding some difficult cases. All of the authorities whose undertakings were accepted by the Secretary of State had indicated an end date for issuing all Section 10 notices before the beginning of April 1982. Those authorities with less than 1,000 notices to issue had all indicated an end date in 1981. Only Cambridge and Chester-le-Street where performance had been questioned at a later stage broke this latter pattern and they had indicated end dates of January 1982 and mid-February 1982 respectively.

4.   Of the 8 authorities initially approached before Norwich where a formal warning had been issued and was still in force in October 1981 two had issued fewer Section 10 notices (Hackney had issued one more); four had issued fewer Section 10 notices when expressed as a percentage of acceptances.

These details are provided in Table 2. What is apparent from this list is that while Norwich may have offered the least satisfactory indications of future progress it does not generally stand out from the other authorities listed.   It would be futile to produce alternative lists or to attempt to suggest that Norwich was not the 'worst offender' in implementing the Right to Buy. Its emergence as the subject of intervention under Section 23 was the result of various complaints and representations and the outcome of discussions and not an analysis of comparative performance based on the kind of data presented here. If we had details of all of the cases where intervention was contemplated we would be in a position to comment on the nature of the judgement made by the Secretary of State in singling out Norwich for action. However, the legislation invites and empowers the Secretary of State to exercise his own judgement over when, where and how to intervene. It does not imply a test of even handedness between local authorities. It is consequently not a remarkable or even critical observation that the pattern of intervention is not justified by comparisons which are not anyway the basis for intervention. However, it is important to note that no clear 'front runner' emerges from such a comparison. This importance is at least in stressing how far the legislation provides powers for the Secretary of State to intervene as he determines rather than on the basis of previously determined objective and visible evidence.

It is not the intention here to attempt to compare Norwich's implementation of the Right to Buy in terms other than those outlined above. It is important however to acknowledge that other authorities adopted procedures which to central government looked like mechanisms for delay. The issue of the legality of using the District Valuer to make initial valuations when the Act placed an appellate function on that office was first highlighted by Greenwich. On the basis of legal advice Greenwich decided they could not use the District Valuer (DV) to make initial valuations. Other authorities including Birmingham accepted this view and the expected rate of processing Section 10 notices reflected this.   A different example emerges if reference is made to authorities which sought to advise tenants of the costs and problems involved in home ownership and insisted on stressing the financial risks

Table 2 : Comparisons of local progress in implementing the Right to Buy

Local Authority	Date of 1st Formal Approach	Acceptances	No of S.10 notices issued by end Oct '81	S.10 Notices as % of acceptances	Indications of Future Progress on issue of S.10 notices	Housing Stock Stock at 1.4.81[4]
Norwich[1]	30.4.81	884	191	22%	all but 101 difficult cases by end June 1982	25300
Tower Hamlets[1]	30.4.81	630	39	6%	631 by April 1982	18400
Islington[1]	11.9.81	707	144	20%	Bulk by January 1982	32100
Copeland[3]	29.10.81	531*	110	21%	531 by May 1982	7800
Chester-le-Street[2]	14.9.81	643	178	28%	630 by 31.1.82	8500
Watford[2]	1.7.81	1295*	153	12%	1265 by 31.12.81	7100
Doncaster[2]	5.2.81	5778	1130	20%	5555 by 1.2.82	38900
Newham[1]	26.2.81	2142	327	15%	2000 by 28.2.82	32200
Salford[2]	11.6.81	2227	484	22%	2100 by 31.12.81	43800
Gateshead[1]	15.4.81	2125	336	16%	2050 by 30.4.82	39300
Cambridge[2]	16.9.81	855	338	40%	831 by 31.1.82	11800
Greenwich[1]	12.11.80	2269	799	35%	2165 by June/July 1982	37400
Leeds[1]	11.2.81	2729	1305	48%	2865 by 1.2.82	97700
Lambeth[1]	4.3.81	807	242	30%	470 houses by 31.12.81 340 flats by end March 82	33400
Hackney[1]	31.3.81	783	192	25%	850 by April/May 1982	28100
Birmingham[1]	29.4.81	4130	1055	26%	3890 by end February 1982	133600

* Figure includes denials

1. Formal warning not withdrawn – timetable not yet agreed.
2. Timetable after formal approach or warning.
3. Discussions still continuing.

4. Figures from DOE Statistics on the Right to Buy. These differ in some cases substantially from those used in the material presented to the court which referred to 1980.

Source: Derived from Department of Environment Evidence to the Divisional Court 17.12.81 and DOE statistics on the Right to Buy.

36

involved. It seems unlikely that a comparative analysis of such detailed procedures would produce any clearer a front runner than comparisons of progress over Section 10 notices. The essence of the procedure was Ministerial judgement. Norwich was the 'victim' of such judgement rather than of unfair or incomplete comparisons. It seems probable that Norwich was a surprise candidate for this role. Greenwich had made the strongest public display and was the most difficult local authority. But they made an acceptable undertaking at the right time.

This situation is what was intended by the legislation. What it gives the Secretary of State is considerable power to single out and pressurise any local housing authorities which have been the subject of complaints received by him. It is a very considerable power to intervene and demand negotiation. Although intervention under Section 23 has been used only rarely (in the Norwich case and subsequently in connection with individual cases in St. Helens and South Northamptonshire) formal warning that the Secretary of State is contemplating using his powers of intervention had been used in 33 cases. And it is in connection with this procedure that the Secretary of State had made formal approaches to 70 authorities and obtained timetable and other undertakings. In this sense Section 23 has not been used as a last resort. It has provided the basis for an unprecedented monitoring, scrutiny and intervention over how local authorities which are not refusing to implement the Right to Buy organise that implementation. It is in the extent of its use rather than the criteria for determining where to intervene that the use of Section 23 bears little comparison with the expectations aroused in the legislative process and the Ministerial assertions that its use would be exceptional.

But the fact that Section 23 was in the legislation was an expression of determination that the Right to Buy should work. The details appear to have been worked out by parliamentary draughtsmen. Ministers expected some local authorities to be hostile or defiant and wanted tenants to alert them to attempts at obstruction. The Right to Buy was their first priority as housing Ministers. They were determined to pursue any complaint or case and regarded Section 23 as both providing the means to implement the spirit of the legislation and obliging them to intervene where obstruction occurred.

It is against this background that the detailed account of the Norwich case should be considered. While the Housing Act provided a very substantial power which was used more generally than anticipated Ministerial action still had to be within the law and the local authority had the right to refer to the courts to test this.

38

3
RELUCTANT COMPLIANCE – PASSIVE RESISTANCE

Norwich City Council did not want to sell council houses. 50 years of Labour dominance had produced a balanced stock of relatively good quality council homes, a housing stock once referred to as the "jewel in the crown" of council housing in the region by Department of the Environment officers. Under discretionary powers, no purpose built council dwellings had been sold. It was not, it was said, so much a matter of principle as a matter of responsible housing management. Labour members were not opposed to owner occupation. Indeed, through local authority mortgages, improvement for sale, building for sale and other such schemes, the council had actively promoted this tenure. And some acquired council dwellings had been sold in the past. If there had been an excess of council houses, if waiting list demand had been satisfied, the council, it was argued, would have sold dwellings as appropriate.

With the election of the Conservative government in 1979, pledged to statutory sales, the decades of local discretion in building, acquisition and disposal were clearly threatened. For a while members chose to ignore, or at least delay, consideration of the statutory provisions contained in the emergent Housing Act. As the day of enactment came closer, it became obvious that some strategic and tactical planning was more advisable than blatant non-compliance or reluctant last minute collaboration. It was recognised that to delay consideration of the provisions of the 1980 Housing Bill until absolutely essential, that is eight weeks after Royal Assent (1 October), would weaken the council's ability to safeguard the council stock within the limits of the law.

Following a series of discussions between leading officers and members, a meeting took place on 15 July 1980 between the Director of Housing and Estates, the Assistant Director of Administration, the Assistant City Treasurer and other officers involved in housing management. The meeting was introduced by the Director of Housing who "outlined the instructions finally and reluctantly given that the officers investigate possible properties at risk under the Housing Bill and see what precautionary measures might be taken to safeguard the council's interests".[1]

It was suggested that the exercise ought to be "tackled quietly" to avoid alarming members and raising issues relating to the broader strategy of the authority. The meeting focused on the provisions for exemption from the Right to Buy contained in the Housing Bill. These exemptions applied mainly to sheltered housing for the elderly. Various schemes within the council stock were discussed, and doubts were expressed as to what would constitute "features that are substantially different from ordinary dwelling houses", one of the qualifications for exemption contained in the Bill. Some schemes had residential staff but no alarm system or communal facilities. Would they qualify? It was noted that in a Good Neighbourhood Scheme for physically handicapped persons "only six out of 18 tenancies at present (were) taken up by families with a physically handicapped member."[2] Would this prejudice the possibility of exemption? At this stage the interpretation of certain clauses in the Bill was ambiguous. But Norwich were keen to maximise the possible exemptions and to safeguard as high a number of council dwellings as possible. Officers were asked to explore exemption for shops held under Part V of the 1957 Housing Act, and thus flats above shops.

Aside from specific exclusions of certain dwelling categories, all other properties held under Part V were eligible for sale. It was noted that this constituted "virtually all the housing stock".[3]

The Bill also excluded properties held and acquired under different statutory powers and this was another route for exemption which was explored at the meeting. Buildings of architectural or historic interest were managed by the Property Committee and were excluded. There was a possibility therefore of transferring a small number of appropriate dwellings out of the pool of general needs housing, and increasing the number of protected properties in this category. It was noted, however, that such "evasive action"[4] could attract the attention of the Secretary of State. For this reason, any such properties should be held under the Norwich Corporation Act (a local Act giving a host of special powers) rather than the Town and Country Planning Act powers and thus made less vulnerable to retaliatory action. The financial counselling service developed by Ipswich for prospective purchasers was also "noted with interest" at this meeting. And there was to be no waiting list for applicants. Those wishing to buy would have to reapply when the Act came into force.

Two days later, the same officers met to consider further the question of exemptions. The room for manoeuvre was very limited. Any significant transfer of dwellings from the Housing Revenue Account would be (and would be seen as) inconsistent with the expressed shortfall of general needs housing contained in HIP submissions to the Department of the Environment. Other forms of safeguard, such as transferring dwellings to housing associations, were also considered, but were ultimately discarded as not being feasible. The discussion continued at a meeting the next day where it was decided to draw up a list of dwellings acquired under improvement policies which might be exempted from the Right to Buy.

The government's Housing Bill came up for discussion at Norwich's Housing Committee on 23 July. The Director of Housing outlined the progress of the legislation and suggested the need to consider those properties "which the committee might wish to protect from compulsory sale".[5] Pat Hollis (the Chair) pointed out that once the Bill became law there were only eight weeks available to set up the necessary administrative machinery. She also told the committee that consideration should be given to appropriating particular properties of architectural or historic interest from Part V to the Corporate Estate. A special meeting of the Housing Committee on 30 July convened for that purpose, and approved the transfer of a number of such properties.

The Housing Act received Royal Assent on 8 August and on 18 August the Housing Committee met to discuss the main provisions of the legislation and to consider the immediate practicalities. The committee considered a detailed paper from Roger Bamford, the Director of Administration and Pat Saunders, the Director of Housing and Estates. This reminded the committee of the current situation regarding enquiries from tenants - tenants being informed at this stage that "it is not the council's policy to sell its housing and [that] applications will not be considered until the relevant part of the Act is in force".[6] Norwich were making it clear to prospective purchasers that any sales were to be under duress and compliance would be reluctant, and only when the Bill became law. The paper to committee made a number of other points. It noted that it was "clearly impossible to estimate the possible level of interest, but even only a 10% response would result in initial enquiries from some 2,400".[7] Interestingly, initial response was much lower than anticipated. By the end of the first year of the Act only some 900 claims to buy had been received representing less than 4% of tenants.[8]

The paper noted that an enquiry had to be distinguished from a notice claiming to exercise the Right to Buy. In the case of the latter, the council would have only four weeks within which to admit or deny the Right to Buy. In parenthesis it noted "although the Act seems to impose no penalty for failure to do so, other than the default powers of the Secretary of State" (our emphasis).[9]

In response to these points and the general description of the legislation, members expressed various views on the subject. Some saw this "as one more example of the erosion of local democracy" and "a transfer of public assets to individuals". Others expressed the view that "the Act merely gave the Right to Buy to those tenants who wished to do so and considered that there was not evidence to show that only the best dwellings would be bought". Pat Hollis commented that the Act was "divisive" and "compelled the diversion of resources to the private sector" and saw it as a threat to the council's previously "balanced" housing policy.[10]

The question of counselling prospective purchasers was discussed. Tenants should be made aware of the commitment they were taking on in entering home ownership. Some of the Conservative members viewed this as a thinly veiled form of deterrence, but they were assured that the "procedure would merely involve making potential buyers aware of the full consequence, particularly since the council might be approached with a view to granting a mortgage".[11] In this context there was some discussion of the relative costs of owning and renting. Tony O'Reilly, the Housing Manager, emphasised the cost of structural repairs which might have to be borne by individuals and a member responded by pointing out that such calculations had to take account of tax rebates and rising values.

The committee was also sensitised to the staffing consequences of administering the Right to Buy. If no additional staff were appointed, other services would inevitably suffer. This was not an acceptable consequence to the majority of members. One way of coping with this was to concentrate sales effort (at least in the early stages) on those properties which represented the greatest administrative burden. For example, Pat Hollis proposed that effort could be directed at enquiries to buy hard to let properties (assuming, of course, that anyone wanted to buy those dwellings). An interesting point was raised with regard to possible abuses of the transfer and exchange system. Could a black market develop where cash might change hands to enable tenants to acquire a more attractive prospect for purchase? Some monitoring was regarded as necessary.

Early in September, the officers met to consider the various adminstrative systems, records and procedures required for the sale of council houses. This covered questions of

- logging and monitoring of individual applications
- exemption from the legislation
- check for secure tenancy
- financial counselling
- monitoring the transfer and exchange system
- communal services in relation to flat sales
- treatment of arrears cases.

Norwich might be reluctant to sell council houses but they were gearing up to carry out the legislation with some degree of diligence.

Two days before the Act came into force, a special meeting of the Housing Committee convened to discuss the broad bands of valuations likely to be used, the implications for transfers and exchanges and staffing generally. A report by the Director of Housing and Estates pointed out that the staff problem was likely to be of a temporary nature in that the majority of applications would be received in the first year. But it was also stressed that the burden of work would fall on those areas where resources were already stretched. There was one vacancy on the legal section but the potential workload was unpredictable. Some authorities were going to make use of private solicitors to deal with much of the conveyancing but the report assumed that "it would not be the Committee's wish to place such legal work outside City Hall".[12] Such an assumption was buttressed by reference to the costs of such services. The use of two to three experienced conveyancers dealing with, say, 500 transactions in a year would cost the council approximately £50,000. This implies a cost of some £100 per transaction. A study commissioned by the Audit Inspectorate and published in 1983 indicated that fees of between £90 and £140 per transaction were payable (in 1981-82) to private solicitors for council house sales with mortgages, compared with an in-house cost of £50 per transaction.[13] These tentative costings suggest that Norwich was accurately assessing such costs.

In the Housing Division there was a possible need for three or four additional staff; a similar number were needed for the Estates Division. Financial counselling, a service Norwich considered essential given its past experience of mortgage difficulties, would need the appointment of one or two temporary staff. In other areas the implications were less certain and would clearly depend on the response to the Right to Buy. All in all the report anticipated the appointment of around ten additional staff.

On valuations, the estates surveyor had made some preliminary calculations concluding that most properties would be valued between £16,000 and £20,000. The report also pointed out the general difficulties of valuing properties in otherwise tenanted areas where there was no precedent, and the need for individual surveys because of the variety of dwelling types which would be involved.

The question of staffing was seen by some members as being in conflict with central government demands to reduce manpower levels in local government. Whilst Pat Hollis, among others, saw the wisdom of financial counselling there seemed to be little justification in boosting staff levels to sell council houses when other areas which might be regarded as having priority were suffering cutbacks. There was a general feeling that there could be no justification for reorienting priorities towards council house sales.

Nevertheless, approval was given to appointment through redeployment of a financial counsellor for a three year period but no other staff were to be appointed to administer the provisions of the Housing Act 1980. The majority view was clearly that staff resources which might enlighten (or discourage?) potential purchasers were a legitimate expense and priority whilst those tasks involved in the mechanism of disposal were no more important than the myriad of responsibilities of a local authority in the field of housing. From the point of view of Norwich, such a position might appear perfectly reasonable but it hardly reflected the hierarchy of priorities of the Conservative government where the sale of council houses held pride of place.

Moreover, the publicity material being sent out to tenants was explicitly antagonistic to the Right to Buy. They were to be informed, for example, that "it would be the policy of any future Labour government to enact legislation which would give local authorities the first option to repurchase council houses when they were resold at a price which would be equal to the original cost price plus inflation and the cost of improvements".[14] Whilst some Conservative members felt that such information was not 'pertinent' at present, it was agreed by the meeting that tenants should be advised accordingly. In a similar vein, the draft information sheet to be distributed with application forms contained the following paragraph:

"however, there is no established market for the resale of former Council houses in Norwich and it remains to be seen whether those advantages will not be as significant as those enjoyed by a home owner in the private sector".[15]

If the Labour government did not get you, the vagaries of the market would! The majority of members, however, felt that this was going too far and this was excluded from the final draft. It is worth noting that other procedures which were later regarded as controversial were not the subject of any extended discussion. Procedures such as broad band valuations and members' approval of disposal of dwellings (rather than delegation to officers) were already firmly established practice.

Just over a month after the Right to Buy came into operation Norwich City Council had received 338 firm applications to buy. One of these was for a two-bedroomed ground floor flat. It was, however, located outside the City Centre and thus outside the area which the committee had agreed should be exempted from the provisions of the Right to Buy. It was nevertheless the kind of property which the council generally regarded as accommodation for the elderly. Norwich saw the provisions in the 1980 Housing Act for exemption of accommodation designed for the elderly as the most exploitable loophole in the legislation. They responded to this request to buy, and others which followed soon after, by widening the exemption to all ground floor flats and referring such applications to the Secretary of State for determination. At the Housing Committee meeting of 19 November when this issue was discussed, a member pointed out that "if the Council took too wide a view of this policy they were less likely to be successful in their application" and suggested that the policy should be applied to City Centre properties only.[16] Pat Hollis, the Chair, responded that there was no reason why all ground floor accommodation should not be regarded as qualifying for exemption.

While this may appear to have been an attempt to exploit these provisions of the Housing Act the circumstances in which these clauses were amended in the House of Commons should not be forgotten. There was a view that a real concession had been won in parliament and that this meant that a large portion of accommodation used by the elderly could be legitimately excluded from the Right to Buy. Such a view was not held by Norwich alone.

Resistance to the policy focused therefore on financial counselling and the search for possible exemptions. This was combined with a certain thoroughness over, for example, valuations and a general concern that priorities in use of staff should not be distorted by sales. There was no question of non-compliance, but a situation was already developing which from one perspective (the local authority) could be seen as a reasonable and studied response to an aggressive piece of legislation but from another (central government) could be viewed as calculated intransigence.

Over the next two or three months, a number of letters were sent to the regional office of the Department of the Environment, listing properties for exemption under Paragraph 5, Schedule 1 of the Housing Act. They pointed out that it was the council's policy and practice to give priority of allocation of ground floor flats to persons of pensionable age or to those having a medical priority. Norwich did not claim that all such flats were occupied by tenants in these categories but that there was excessive demand from elderly persons for suitable accommodation due to the demographic structure of the city. The council pointed out to the DOE that:

> "The lettings practice which is attempting to meet this rising level of need is established and operative and is well proved by the fact that, for example, from a total of 153 ground floor flats in that area (central area) 114 are now occupied by persons of pensionable age".[17]

Not only was this presented as well-established council policy but the various letters seeking exemptions argued that this was as consistent with government policy as council house sales in that:

> "The Secretary of State has made it very clear on a number of occasions that he expects the emphasis of local authority housing programmes to be concerned with those having special needs. In this respect the Council is endeavouring to achieve that end".[18]

DOE responded to each application by requesting additional information. Under which Act were the properties acquired? Were there any other grounds for exemption such as the tenants not being secure as defined by the legislation? And in a questioning tone "I gather from the correspondence to hand that the Council would be unwilling to sell these properties voluntarily".[19]

Subsequently DOE asked to be satisfied that the dwellings sought for exemption had been constructed as Category 1 dwellings or evidence that they had been specifically designed or adapted for occupation by persons of pensionable age. In addition, the Director of Housing or Deputy Director had to sign a statement which read "....it is the practice of the City of Norwich to let (the address of the particular dwelling should be inserted) only for occupation by persons of pensionable age". Norwich was also asked to give tenancy details such as age on initial allocation, for each dwelling. The DOE had also written to the tenants concerned "asking if they wish to comment on the Council's application".[20]

A number of such requests were received by Norwich. After some consideration they replied to the various queries at the end of April. The key problem for the council was that the majority of exemptions requested did not concern dwellings specifically designed for occupation by persons of pensionable age. Neither were they only available for letting to such categories of applicant.

In response to the first point, Norwich offered an alternative definition of design and referred "the Secretary of State to the Oxford Dictionary definition which had received judicial approval in previous legal cases". This defined designed as "set apart for, destined or intended". On this definition it was suggested "siting and location are clearly as significant an aspect of design as the architectural features of a building". Following this logic, it was then argued that "the mere fact that a flat is situated on the ground floor of a block is sufficient to satisfy the design requirements of the legislation".

On the second point, whilst Norwich could not claim that only persons of pensionable age were offered such dwellings, "it was the Council's policy to give priority to elderly applicants and those having medical priority".[21]

Meanwhile, both the financial counselling and the valuation procedures were proving to be extremely time consuming. By 11 February the council had received 1,204 enquiries from tenants and 559 firm applications. Around 90 applicants had been given financial counselling and of those a third had positively expressed their intention to proceed to completion. Just under 500 applications had been passed to the Estates Division for broad band valuations and 116 had been returned. It was noted that "there was a general feeling that the turnround of applications for Broad Banding ought to be quickened if the administration was not soon to be inundated with applicants' queries of an unproductive nature".[22]

Concern with progress was increasingly preoccupying Tory members of the council who regularly asked for details of the processing of applications. And towards the end of February Norwich received a letter from DOE detailing complaints from two tenants about "apparent lack of progress". The council was asked to provide information on the dates of the applications and when they expected to be able to issue notices of purchase price to the tenants.[23] This was to be the first of many such letters detailing tenants' complaints over lack of progress. These letters suggested among other things that the council was employing "delaying tactics, dragging its heels"; that financial counselling consisted of "pointing out the disadvantages of being a home owner"; and that the rate of progress meant that it could take years for some tenants to complete purchase.[24] Some tenants also referred to unreasonable covenants being part of the conveyance. For example, Clause II of the conveyance was an undertaking "To permit the Council and its duly authorised agents with or without tools or appliances at all reasonable times to enter upon the property to view the state and conditions...."

This barrage of tenants' complaints appears to have been encouraged by the local Conservative Party which held public meetings on the subject, and Conservative Party Central Office, by a series of articles which appeared in the local press and by more frequent questions in Housing Committee by Tory members concerning overall progress on sales. It is worth noting that complaints were from only a minority of applicants and few went to Norwich itself. The council could therefore have legitimately regarded this as the politically inspired orchestration of the complaints of the few rather than the representation of a majority concern.

On 3 March, Councillor Mercer, a Conservative member, requested information from Pat Hollis, Chair of the Housing Committee, about the number of applications to buy so far received, and the number of response notices confirming or denying the Right to Buy which had been issued. And he added "Since many applications

48

have now been pending for some five months, will she (Pat Hollis) also tell the Council how many valuations have been completed and how many Section 10 Purchase Price Notices have been issued?" He also pointed out that "in carrying out these valuations rapidly will the Chairman take note of the observations of the Housing Minister, Mr John Stanley, that there is absolutely no excuse for local authorities to claim that they are short staffed since they can use private valuers for a fee per house of around £30, or they can use the services of the District Valuers, who, we are assured, are happy to oblige and whose services will cost the local authority and the tenants nothing at all".[26]

Pat Hollis replied that "To date 1,255 enquiries have been made resulting in the return of 591 applications from tenants wishing to buy their Council property and leading to the issue of 501 response notes. No valuations have been formally approved...." In noting Councillor Mercer's additional comments concerning the use of private valuers or the DV she reminded him "of the resolution of Housing Committee on 1 October 1980 ....that no work arising from the implementation of the provisions of the Housing Act 1980 would be placed with outside firms".[27]

The next day the Eastern Evening News reported Councillor Mercer's question as a "Blast over 'delay' in home sales".[28] And an article in the same newspaper towards the end of April carried the headline "Dossier of despair bid in buy-your-home row".[29] This referred to comments by a "spokesman for Mr Michael Heseltine's department" who was quoted as saying:

> "The matter, to some extent, is in the hands of the tenants. The more they draw attention to councils not satisfying their wishes, the more likely action from the government will be brought. If tenants are feeling frustrated the best thing they can do is put pen to paper and let us know about it".[30]

In the same article Len Stevenson, the Leader of the council, responded to the view that Norwich was purposely dragging its feet in implementing the Right to Buy by arguing the admittedly slow rate of progress was a combination of staff shortages and the overall pattern of priorities. But such a view received little sympathy with Councillor Mercer who, in the final paragraph of the article suggested that tenants were being "swindled" and that there was "a growing groundswell of resentment among them". Such a "groundswell of resentment" evidenced by tenants putting "pen to paper" proved a crucial aspect of the subsequent court proceedings. Under the provisions of the Housing Act 1980, the powers of intervention hinged more on proof of households experiencing unreasonable delays in buying their dwellings rather than the "reasonableness" of the council in deciding its overall system of priorities. The encouragement to tenants to "put pen to paper" therefore was of more than symbolic value. A "dossier of despair" from tenants was not just "more likely" to bring action from the government: it was a legal precondition for intervention. This was an aspect of the framing of the legislation. Given the Ministers' total commitment to the Right to Buy it was also likely to prompt Ministerial action.

Two days after this article, on 1 May, Norwich received a letter from the DOE in London which was noticeably less muted in its concern over slow progress. As well as requesting the usual details of numbers of sales and procedures adopted, Ian Edye, the Regional Controller at DOE, had been 'instructed' to draw the attention of Norwich to Section 10(1) of the Housing Act which detailed the duty of public landlords to serve <u>as soon as practicable</u> a notice on tenants whose Right to Buy had been established which detailed among other things, the value and purchase price of the dwelling. The letter added "as you know, the Secretary of State has a power under S23 of the Act to intervene where it appears to him that tenants generally or a tenant or tenants of a particular landlord have or may have difficulty in exercising the right to buy effectively and expeditiously".[31]

The phoney war it seems was over and Norwich was fast emerging as a frontrunner for intervention by central government.

4
CONFLICT AND NEGOTIATION

Correspondence

The senior officers concerned with the sales issues met on 5 May to discuss the agenda for the forthcoming meeting of the Mortgages (Joint) Sub-Committee. Enquiries from prospective purchasers had continued to come in at the rate of around 40 per week. The total was now 1,468, still a relatively small proportion of the tenant population. Firm applications to buy had declined from a peak of 60 per week to 15, an overall total of 905. 22 offers had been sent out. At this stage 186 applicants had been given financial counselling.

There was some discussion of the valuations referred to the District Valuer (DV) which had reduced the values determined by the council by between £2,000 and £3,000. It was noted that it "would be for the Committee to decide whether his (District Valuer) valuations should automatically be reflected in future applications relating to accommodation of the same type".[1]

On general matters, the committee would have to discuss the recent letter from DOE which "in effect, singled out the City for critical examination of the effectiveness of its sales policy".[2] In addition, the NALGO AGM had passed a recent resolution opposing sales in principle and giving Branch support to any members who might refuse to cooperate with the sale of council houses. But NALGO NEC would not sanction unlawful action.

In considering the criticism of the council by the DOE, the Director of Housing summarised the main points which had been made in response:

"It has been pointed out to the Department that:

1. We have no experience of selling Council houses.

51

2. We are expected to reduce staff, and have therefore taken on only one additional person to deal with the considerable additional work.

3. Even if we used the services of the DV, the workload would be only marginally reduced.

4. If the Council used private valuers we would not be able to recover their costs.

5. Our record since the 1980 Act came into force is no different from most local authorities - at least in the region....

6. That the Council is abiding by the letter of the law and all statutory time limits are being adhered to.

Nonetheless, the Secretary of State has decided to take the first step in naming Norwich for being, in his opinion, too slow in dealing with sales".

The memo ended with the comment that "all it means at the moment presumably is that the Department will take an even greater interest in our progress".[3]

The council view was that if Norwich was slow in selling council houses it was because it was a new policy for them and they were concerned to implement it properly with due concern for the ratepayers. Resources were stretched and the use of the DV or outside valuers as suggested by DOE would be either only of marginal benefit or an unreasonable use of council finances. At this stage the objections to use of the DV were in terms of value for money rather than on legal grounds. Moreover, they were no worse than any other authority in the region. At that stage the highest sellers in the region were Great Yarmouth and Peterborough with six completed sales each. The situation therefore, according to the Director of Housing, was one in which Norwich was coping reasonably within the law.

Such a view again contrasted with the article which had appeared a few days earlier in the Norwich Mercury. Under the headline "When will Norwich Council Sell Up?" Councillor Mercer's concern that sales were being "deliberately thwarted" and that Labour was "trying to frighten people off" was well publicised. It was according to the Norwich Mercury "A question 904 city people were asking". Councillor Mercer claimed that Norwich "was not complying with the spirit (our emphasis) of the law" and that "there are an awful lot of angry people". Later in the article, Pat Hollis echoed the views of the Director of Housing that "The Council is obeying the law as the law requires it" but added that people "should recognise the reasons and the very real complications and restraints caused by lack of staff".[4]

Whether the question "When will Norwich sell up?" was preoccupying 904 people is unknown but letters from tenants continued to arrive on the desks of John Stanley and Michael Heseltine and even Margaret Thatcher.

Some tenants pointed out that the Conservative government was responsible for the rapid rise in rents but that the escape route of purchase was being kept closed by recalcitrant Labour councils like Norwich:

"Is HM Government ruling the country or councils like the Norwich City Council ....?"[5]

Some took the view that Norwich's resistance was rather covert:

"Unlike some Labour-controlled councils, Norwich has kept a low profile over the sale of council houses, and it might be supposed that these are proceeding normally".[6]

Many pointed to the projected delays in reaching completion at the present rate of progress:

"At the rate the council are working it seems that some people may have to wait nearly seven years before they can buy".[7]

And financial counselling was a common source of complaint:

"....I was summoned to the City Hall for a 'Councilling' which consisted of pointing out the disadvantages of being a home owner".[8]

".... had an interview a few weeks ago (another ploy of delaying the sale) in which all the bad points were put to you. Also you would be moved out of your home if you couldn't keep up the payments".[9]

One correspondent claimed that:

> "The most vicious Councillor is a Mrs Pat Hollis who
> has openly stated that council houses will be sold 'over
> my dead body'."[10]

The possibility of direct intervention by central government was
clearly in many people's minds:

> "....for God's sake send some one here who will carry
> out the law of the land so justice is done to the citizens
> of Norwich".[11]

As mentioned earlier, some of these letters were probably
prompted by articles in the local press and the activity of the local
Conservative Party. One tenant went so far as to organise a
petition alleging slow progress on sales, which contained 460
signatures. The signatories threatened to withdraw rents and stage
demonstrations. It should be borne in mind that while the
consequences of delay for these potential purchasers were that
they continued to pay rents (and these rents were increasing) the
valuation date had been fixed last August (1980). Purchase price
therefore was not affected by delay.

At the Housing Committee Meeting of 13 May, sales progress was
discussed and particularly the questions of why Norwich had been
singled out for attention when its rate of sale was no worse than
many other authorities. The explanation offered by the Director of
Housing was that it was not so much the number of completions
which was at issue but the level of valuations in proportion to the
total number of applications. On a comparable basis Norwich was
certainly falling behind on this criterion. It was agreed to increase
the number of valuations by 50%, from 12 to 18 per month, as they
were becoming more a matter of routine.

On 20 May, the agreed response was sent to Ian Edye, the Regional
Controller at DOE. This supplied the requested statistical data on
applications and valuations, as well as outlining the procedures
adopted by the council in processing applications. It was the issue
of counselling and the use of the District Valuer which were the
main points of disagreement between the DOE and the council.
The letter described the 'broad band' valuations carried out by the
council's valuers as "a preliminary estimate of the likely value of
each property, based on an external inspection only, and its purpose
is to give tenants an early indication of the probable price of their
property". It went on:

"This information is provided at a discussion of the proposed purchase, to which each applicant is invited and given the opportunity to raise any problems or queries. I recognise that this is not part of the required statutory process, but there is no doubt that most tenants have found it to be very useful".[12]

To counteract the charge that such a procedure could be construed as a measure introduced to delay progress on sales it was pointed out that:

"This has always been the Council's standard practice, because it is considered that it would be contrary to the interests of the ratepayers as a whole if the Council's property assets were to be disposed of without the terms having been agreed by its elected members".[13]

Whilst admitting that such a procedure involved a certain amount of delay this was attributed to the lack of experience of the City Council in selling council houses and difficulty caused by the requirements of the 1980 Act. The involvement of members in the valuations of disposals was argued, however, to be proper and responsible and the frequency of meetings of the Mortgages (Joint) Sub-Committee had been increased to clear some of the backlog.

The question of using the District Valuers to speed up the rate of valuations was, it seems, less open to compromise:

"The Council takes the view that such a costly practice would, in reality, save little time. It would still be necessary for the Council to prepare and supply the background information on which individual valuations depend and it is this part of the valuation process which is by far the most time consuming element. As far as the District Valuer is concerned, the Council would also question the propriety of referring voluntarily to him cases on which, at a later stage, he might be asked to arbitrate".[14]

Throughout this time Norwich continued to receive a regular flow of letters from the DOE's Eastern Regional Office listing members of the public in Norwich who had complained about lack of progress on their applications. In replying to these now routine requests for information Norwich stressed a lack of experience in selling council houses as the main factor in delay and emphasised that more rapid progress was being made. Norwich was, however, reluctant to offer any precise dates for the issue of formal offers to tenants - those near to the top of the list would be notified "within the next few months".[15]

The rules of engagement were, however, about to change. The tactical battle carried on over the previous months through correspondence was to give way to a more direct form of confrontation.

Direct confrontation

On 16 June Norwich received a rather more formal communication from Ian Edye, at DOE Eastern Regional Office:

> "In the light of the information given in your letter, I am to tell you that Ministers remain dissatisfied with the rate of progress by your authority in implementing the right to buy provisions of Chapter 1 of Part 1 of the Housing Act 1980. There is a number of points on which Ministers wish to have further information and I am, therefore, to invite you here to a meeting in the near future to discuss them. I shall be in touch with you to arrange a convenient time".[16]

The letter went on to request information regarding the valuation procedure. In particular, it was concerned with the frequency of meetings of the Mortgages (Joint) Sub-Committee and the extent to which the council's procedure of involving members directly in the valuation process affected the time taken to process applications. The council was reminded that Section 10 notices making formal offers were to be served as soon as practicable.

As regards the reluctance of Norwich to use the District Valuer, Edye found it:

> "odd that your Council should consider such a procedure costly, since the services of the District Valuer are available to the Council for such work without charge. I wonder, too, whether your arrangements imply an overestimate of the amount of information which the valuer will need in order to make the valuation. You have not listed the items of information which you normally provide but other authorities have found it possible to make more rapid progress by altering their

procedures so as to provide rather less information than they had at first provided".[17]

Apart from cost factors, Norwich had objected to the use of the District Valuer because of his appellate role should there be appeals against initial valuations. It was objected that circumstances could arise where the District Valuer was determining an appeal (under Section 11 of the Act) against his own valuation. On this point Edye reassured the council:

> "I do not think that there is any reason for the Council to be concerned on this score. Ministers remain confident that the District Valuer will provide an independent and impartial determination whatever the circumstances under which he is carrying out the valuation. In no case will the particular valuer who values the house under Section 6 be allowed to make a Section 11 determination relating to the same house. To ensure a fresh and impartial approach, one of the two most senior members of the office - the District Valuer personally or his Deputy - will make the determination under Section 11. Ministers do not, therefore, accept that it would be in any way prejudicial to employ the District Valuer to carry out initial valuations".[18]

On 3 July Peter Rosson, the Assistant Director of Administration, wrote to Edye accepting the invitation to a meeting. This was arranged for 9 July. An earlier meeting had been requested by DOE but this had proved impossible. Moreover, Rosson pointed out that the extra time would allow the council to review its procedures in the light of the Ministers' misgivings. These misgivings were no doubt reinforced by the statistical information included. By that date 916 applications to buy had been received. Only 53 Section 10 offers had been issued and no sales had been completed. But the letter went on to reassure Ministers that "Although no sales have yet been completed, the first are imminent and those precedents having been established, I see no reason from the Council's point of view, why future sales should not proceed speedily to completion once the conveyancing stage has been reached".[19]

The careful planning and the setting up of the appropriate administrative machinery was it seems going to pay off in the end. But speeding sales to completion was not going to be aided by the

District Valuer. The fact that this procedure had been adopted by other authorities and that progress had been accelerated by streamlining the amount of information supplied to the District Valuer remained an unconvincing argument to Norwich. As Rosson put it:

> "I am particularly intrigued by the fact that other authorities have apparently been able to make more rapid progress by supplying the District Valuer with reduced information".

And added, with a not immodest amount of sarcasm:

> "My Council would be most interested to learn how this can be achieved without the danger of prejudicing the interests of both the purchaser and the local authority. In our experience, it has proved necessary to carry out full inspections of each property, to an extent which is possibly even greater than that associated with the more conventional form of house sales because we are concerned with the sub-division and sale of developments which were not designed with such a prospect in mind".[20]

These issues were discussed at a meeting on 8 July. Saunders informed the meeting of the impending visit by representatives of the DOE. Could completions be increased and what were the attitudes of members towards the use of the District Valuer given the pressure being placed on Norwich? One way of speeding up progress was to take the relatively straightforward cases first leaving the more complicated properties, such as flats, until later. It was felt, however, that this would inevitably involve taking cases out of order, would upset applicants and generate even more complaints. Whether or not Ministers and the DOE would have been satisfied with numbers of completions achieved rather than being over concerned with the order in which applications were being processed was not discussed. It was another example of Norwich taking what could be seen as a correct and responsible position but one likely to exacerbate rather than alleviate disagreements with the DOE and Ministers. And there was no movement on the question of using the District Valuer, the Chair (now Councillor Fullman) again pointing out that "if there was an appeal against a valuation, the District Valuer would be asked to arbitrate".[21] The furthest Norwich would go in satisfying the demands of the DOE was to increase the number of cases coming to the Mortgages (Joint) Sub-Committee from 20 to 30 per month.

The next day officers of the council met officers from the Department of the Environment. The DOE was represented by Peter Rumble, Under Secretary; Ian Edye, the Regional Controller and Nicholas Jones from Eastern Region office. The Norwich officers were Pat Saunders, the Director of Housing; Tony O'Reilly, the Housing Manager; Bob Camp, the Assistant Estates Surveyor; Peter Rosson, the Assistant Director of Administration and Peter Mason, the Senior Legal Assistant.

The meeting began with Peter Rumble reiterating that the Minister was dissatisfied with the performance of Norwich City Council. He pointed out that it was "totally unacceptable that the rate of service of Notices under Section 10 of the Housing Act, 1980 should be a mere three per week...."[22] Rumble then warned that if the situation did not improve there could be direct intervention by the Secretary of State under Section 23. He required clear information on what measures the council was prepared to take to permit tenants to exercise their Right to Buy; what changes in existing procedures would take place to facilitate this end; and a precise timetable on the intended throughput of sales in accordance with the Act.

Saunders stated that Norwich did not exactly enthuse over council house sales but was nevertheless obliged and committed to act according to the law. But the lack of experience in selling council houses and the absence of the bureaucratic machinery had meant delays. Those involved in sales were now, however, gaining that experience and the processing of applications had been increased by over 150%. Given existing procedures and staffing levels it would be expected that the council could deal with 30 cases per month. Saunders would not extend this prediction to a definite figure on completed sales per month which was, of course, what the DOE and Ministers wanted. Other authorities under similar pressures had tended to comply with DOE set targets - whether they were feasible or not. As was consistently the case, Norwich were both rigorous and provocative in maintaining the difficulty of predicting rates of completion. Saunders pointed out that the speed of completion depended on the purchaser's solicitors and not on any action of the council. This was partly true. Whilst certain aspects of the conveyancing process were outside the control of the council the rate of initial processing of applications by the council inevitably set the limits on likely levels of completions over, say, a year. In this context, Peter Rumble was quick to reply that even at the increased rate of 30 cases per month it would take two years for all offers to be made on the current backlog of applications. Again, he emphasised the likelihood of direct intervention if Norwich could not do better and added that "other authorities which were slow to carry out their obligations under the Act had by now achieved a better record than Norwich City Council was contemplating at the present time".[23]

The discussion then shifted to a consideration of the valuation procedures. Why bother with broad band valuations at consultation stage rather than providing a valuation for each dwelling early in the process? The suspicion here was that the two stage valuation was not only a delaying tactic but a way of deterring would-be purchasers who might assume that their house would be more expensive to buy than would in fact be the case. There was also a more general concern that the involvement of members in the details of disposals and valuations was unnecessary and time consuming. In fact the drop-out rate was low and, Rumble was told, members insisted on this procedure. Norwich reiterated that members had always been involved in the disposal of land owned by the City Council. This was not a procedure introduced for the Right to Buy. On the contrary, there were no delegated powers to officers in this area because of the need for local democratically elected members to concern themselves with protecting the assets of ratepayers.

Three options on how the valuation process could be improved were then outlined by Rumble. Firstly, the District Valuer could be used. Saunders replied that "the use of the District Valuer was not considered appropriate since ultimately the same information would be required before the sales could proceed".[24] Secondly, more staff in City Hall could be allocated to work on the Right to Buy. This was not possible because of existing workloads. Thirdly, the private sector could be used. This had been ruled out, argued Saunders, because of cost considerations. Taking everything into account, given present staffing levels and workloads in other policy areas "no department could deal with more than 30 applications at any one time".[25] And a suggested figure of 70 applications per month far exceeded the feasible target.

Rumble then summarised the points he would be reporting to the Minister and reaffirmed his dissatisfaction with the council's proposals. All Section 10 notices, he said, "should be completed within a very few months".[26] When challenged to be more specific he declined but suggested that intervention was likely unless 160 cases per month were being processed. Given what had been said previously this was clearly out of the question.

It was not long after this meeting that Norwich received a formal warning from Marsham Street. On 28 July, Peter Rumble wrote to Tony Glover, the Chief Executive:

> "Ministers regard the proposed rate of progress as unacceptable. They have noted that over 800 tenants have had their right to buy admitted and that only just over 50 as at 30th June had had their dwellings valued and notices under Section 10 issued. At a rate of 30 valuations per month it would be well over 2 years from now before Section 10 notices were issued in respect of those tenants where the right to buy has already been admitted and about 3 years after the right to buy provisions of the Housing Act came into force. There would subsequently be further stages following the issue of the Section 10 notice before the property could be conveyed to the tenant.

> I now write to give formal warning that the Secretary of State is contemplating giving your authority notice of his intention to use his powers under Section 23 of the Housing Act 1980 to enable your authority's tenants to exercise the right to buy and the right to a mortgage".[27]

On the same day in the House of Commons, David Mellor, Conservative Member for Wandsworth fed John Stanley the question:

> "What further steps is he taking regarding those authorities where he is still contemplating use of his powers of intervention under Section 23 of the Housing Act 1980?"

Stanley replied:

> "My right hon. Friend is today sending letters to the following authorities stating that he is contemplating intervention under Section 23 of the Housing Act 1980:

>> Gateshead, Hackney, Leeds, Leicester, Norwich, Sunderland and Watford.

> A further five authorities to whom my right hon. Friend sent similar letters a few weeks ago have now given precise undertakings as to their timetables for processing the right to buy applications which they have

received. In the light of these undertakings, and other measures these five authorities are taking, my right hon. Friend has written to them today to inform them that he has decided not to intervene at the present time. He will continue to monitor carefully whether the tenants of these authorities have or may have difficulty in exercising their right to buy effectively and expeditiously and whether these authorities are fulfilling their undertakings within the timetables which they have given. These five authorities are:

Barnsley, Burnley, Middlesbrough, Walsall and Waltham Forest".[28]

One of the more bizarre and difficult to evaluate episodes in the saga occurred at this stage. On 8 August the Prime Minister, Margaret Thatcher, visited Norwich to see a local manufacturing success story (subsequently liquidated). Mrs Thatcher also had a meeting with local Conservative Party workers and hoped to meet some of the people who had bought the first few council houses. Mrs Thatcher was reported to be astonished that the City had not sold any dwellings and told Party supporters that the City could end up in the firing line on this issue. Mrs Thatcher is reported to have pledged to take the issue up with Secretary of State, Michael Heseltine.[29]

The Minister of Housing and Construction

The meeting with the Department of the Environment and the formal warning of possible intervention under Section 23 raised the temperature in City Hall. Members decided that a direct approach to the Minister was the only way to communicate the impossibility of meeting the threatened target of completions. As background, officers were requested to analyse and detail the staffing and other implications of completing the backlog of more than 700 applications by the end of the calendar year. Options to be considered, subject to union approval, ranged from staff overtime to the re-employment of retired members of staff. Another possibility might be the abandonment of the Mortgages (Joint) Sub-Committee and full delegation of authority to the Chairman to approve valuations.

At a council meeting on 12 August, Tony O'Reilly, the Housing Manager, informed members that the first completions were likely to be achieved within a week or two. Delays, however, were being

MAGGIE: HOMES SALES HINT

THE FACT that Norwich City Council has not sold a single council house since the new Housing Act came into force last October has brought top-level astonishment — from Prime Minister Margaret Thatcher.

But as she warned that Norwich could be top of the Government's "hit-list" of councils not making good progress on the issue, city Labour officials accused her of interfering.

They are seeking a meeting with Environment Minister Mr. Michael Heseltine to thrash the matter out.

That meeting has not yet been fixed, but it seems that Mrs. Thatcher may well have a word with Mr. Heseltine first, for she told Conservative Party workers in Norwich during her visit last week that she would immediately take up the issue with him.

After her private meeting with party workers the Norwich North Conservative

by Terry Reeve

chairman, Mr. Conal Gregory, said:

"She was actually hoping to meet some of the people who had bought the first few houses. The fact that the city had not sold a single one astonished her."

He said Mrs. Thatcher told them she would ensure Norwich was at the forefront of measures against councils who do not conform to the right-to-buy rules, if the Government did not see action from the city.

As reported last week, Mr. Heseltine has told the council it must sell over 800 homes by the end of the year or face action from the Government which has the power to appoint a commissioner to handle the sales operation if it finds a council has been deliberately dragging its feet.

The housing committee

chairman, Mr. David Fullman, said they were hoping to meet Mr. Heseltine and Housing Minister Mr. John Stanley, but by coming out with her statement, "probably with very little background and briefing," Mrs. Thatcher was "antagonising people and possibly throwing a spanner in the works."

But Mr. Fullman agreed that if Mr. Heseltine was prepared to come to some agreement on the matter, "it is possible the sales process could be speeded up."

If he was adamant that 800 houses should be sold by the end of the year, it would mean closing down half the management section to deal with it, however, Mr. Fullman said.

At present the council was carrying out an exercise to see if what Mr. Heseltine was demanding was feasible.

"At the conveyancing stage we will push sales through as quickly as possible," he said.

House sales 'within weeks'

The first council house sale in Norwich is expected to be completed "within a few weeks."

City housing and estates director, Mr. Pat Saunders, made the prediction yesterday in answer to some tenants' fears over delays.

"Our solicitors expect the first sale within a few weeks and then we expect them to come through every week," he said.

At least 46 cases were currently in the hands of council or clients' solicitors and a number of tenants had accepted the price. Detailed matters were now being discussed and no actual completion had yet been made.

DOCUMENTS

Mr. Saunders' comments came after some tenants had expressed fears over the time taken to complete the sales.

One, Mr. David Smith, of 2, Stone Road, Norwich, said he went to the city council in the hope of buying his home last October, when the right-to-buy rules were introduced, and is waiting for the council to contact him for the completion documents, after accepting the valuation.

His solicitor has constantly been in touch with the legal department of the council and was recently told the situation was in hand and he would be hearing from them, he said.

"I'm just waiting on them," said Mr. Smith, whose mortgage is ready and who has been eager to buy his home for the past nine years.

Heseltine threat on city house sales

NORWICH City Council has been added to Michael Heseltine's "hit list" of authorities which are not selling off council houses quickly enough.

Norwich is one of seven authorities now being threatened with action as a result of alleged "go slow" policies, and this could mean that the Government sends in a commissioner to take over the controversial operation.

Mr. David Ennals, MP for Norwich North, revealed yesterday that the city was in trouble after receiving a copy of a House of Commons reply given by the Minister of Housing and Construction in the Department of the Environment, Mr. John Stanley, on Tuesday night.

BACKED DOWN

It said Mr. Heseltine was sending letters to the offending authorities telling them he was contemplating action under the Housing Act, 1980.

Mr. Ennals said five authorities previously warned on the same count had now backed down and

agreed to toe the line, but the issue was still open with regard to five more.

Yesterday he criticised the way the Commons answer was given on the Tuesday night before the Royal Wedding, and in the final week of Parliament when there was not time for it to be challenged.

"This is another example of the way in which the Government hopes the action it is taking won't be noticed," he said. "The Secretary of State grossly overestimated the number of people who would be interested in purchasing. Now he is desperately trying 'by threats to have some figures added on to sales which won't look so derisory."

PRIORITY

Mr. Ennals said the Government would not be able to inflict any financial punishment on Norwich "other than that it was already operating."

Mr. Ennals said the council had not tried to defy the law, but it had given the sale of council houses a low priority, and was not speeding up the process as this would involve taking on staff and cost money. Only 3.3 per cent of tenants had shown any interest in buying their houses.

"Money is tight," said Mr.

Ennals. "Mr. Heseltine is also telling the council they have got to cut down on expenditure and reduce manpower."

Mr. David Fullman, chairman of the city housing committee, said the council had not yet received the letter.

"But I wouldn't agree with the criticism," he said. "It is a question of priority. Our first priority is proper management of the stock. We can't sell any more at the moment without taking on extra staff.

"If Mr. Heseltine brought someone in it would be a complete negation of local democracy. We were elected to run the city in the way we believe is best. Heseltine is dabbling in and trying to run it from London — or Toxteth at present."

FULL STOP

WITH good sense and lucidity, the Master of the Rolls, Lord Denning, has delivered what we trust will be the definitive judgment in the case of Norwich City Council v Mr. Heseltine. Responsibility for the "intolerable delay" met by some tenants seeking to buy their homes lay with the council; councillors had been "badly advised"; the council was "misguided" and had no answer for it. The three Appeal Court judges could scarcely have been more dismissive of the council's case. City Hall's campaign of frustration and, it would appear, dissimulation has taken its toll of time, public money and civic reputation. Let it now, as Lord Denning has suggested, speed up sales and so demonstrate its competence to manage without the presence of Whitehall nominees.

63

caused by legal difficulties over properties with shared access and more significantly by the increasing number of applicants seeking a revaluation by the District Valuer. For example, more than half the applicants receiving Section 10 approvals the previous month had replied by requesting a revaluation. The meeting coincided with a consideration of how best to react to the letter of the 28 July from Ian Edye. It was decided to send two replies - one to the DOE and a personal letter from the Leader of the council to the Minister. There was a strong feeling that Ministers were reacting to what members saw as a misrepresentation of their stance and attitudes on sales. As David Fullman recalls "the general drift....was maintained that we would meet the government part way all the time.... It was pretty obvious that there had been some correspondence between him (the Minister) and local Tories and they had misread the situation and reported us as having a completely uncompromising attitude...."[30] In the same vein Tony Glover, the Chief Executive stressed that:

> "There was never any question about not complying with the law but there was a question of speed and....resources. The council always said that it intended to comply with the law and the Leader of the council, Mr Stevenson, said that over and over again".[31]

On 13 August Tony Glover conveyed similar comments to Peter Rumble at Marsham Street. After providing the statistics on progress (no completions as yet but some under way) he pointed out that the threatened targets were quite unrealistic, outside the scope of the legislation and the council had a range of obligations which had to be met within limited resources:

> "You ask for the date by which it is intended that Section 10 offer notices will be issued in respect of the applications still outstanding, but you restrict the scope of the possible reply by stating that "Ministers would expect that date to be before the end of the present calendar year". You also say that Ministers expect the weekly rate of completions to be not less than the weekly rate of agreeing terms.
>
> This is the point at which, with the greatest respect, it seems that Ministers may have misunderstood the City Council's approach towards the implementation of the right to buy provisions of the Act and the implications of attempting to comply with such targets which, apart

from being quite unreasonable, appear to rest on no foundation in the law".

Stressing the fact that Norwich was implementing the Right to Buy but within its overall system of priorities he argued that:

"the Council has always been firmly committed to complying with the Act and, furthermore, that the position which it has reached is not a result of dilatoriness, as your letter implies. This Council is a responsible authority implementing the Act as efficiently as it reasonably can within the limits of its resources and its obligations to tenants who wish to buy, to those who do not, and to the ratepayers as a whole. The Council has had no previous experiences of selling its housing stock and could not, therefore, have been expected to respond to the Act's requirements as rapidly as authorities with a tradition of voluntary sales and readily adaptable systems and procedures".[32]

Returning to an argument used by Norwich in the past, Glover suggested that not only was the council implementing the law reasonably in terms of its overall responsibilities in other areas but its policies were in sympathy with central government priorities on the rational and efficient use of local resources:

"The question of resources is, of course, important. The Council is mindful of the Government's overall policy that public sector manning levels should be contained and, where possible, reduced and has so far consciously sought to avoid employing additional staff. On the other hand, the expertise which has had to be called upon for house sales is already engaged on areas where the Council's continuing obligations remain substantial and indeed have, in some respects, been increased by other demands of central government. The growing task of the local authority in stimulating local employment opportunities and the need to respond to the sudden and substantial increase in eligibility for rent rebates are but two examples".

His letter continued:

"The Council must, therefore, necessarily balance the demands of the right to buy provisions against other no less compelling demands on its resources during a period of increasing constraints. This is a question of judgement. It is wrong to imply, as your letter does, that the Council's judgements have been unreasonable. The use of valuation and legal services from the private sector would only reduce further the level of the Council's resources, while the Council has made its view clear that the suggested use of the District Valuer would not only save little time over all, but would also be improper because of the appellate role which the Act lays upon him.

The Council remains convinced that its approach to the task is what should be expected from any responsible authority and, while the need to make the initial preparations has meant that comparatively few offers have been made so far, the rate of progress has increased and is increasing.

These factors have always made it difficult to provide reliably accurate estimates of the date by which the backlog of applications will be cleared. I would suggest that they also make it unreasonable to draw any conclusions from a mere extrapolation from either past or present rates of activity.

Members of my Council have seen your letter of 28 July and you should know that they are so concerned by the view that Ministers appear to be taking of the position in Norwich that the leader of the Council and the Chairman of its Housing Committee have written to the Secretary of State seeking an urgent meeting with him. I am sure that it is in the interests of all concerned that such a meeting should take place".[33]

This letter encapsulated the main points of disagreement between Norwich and central government. It was a matter of priorities not a matter of noncompliance. Whilst for Ministers the Right to Buy was the high profile policy demanding a high priority in its implementation, for Norwich there were more pressing concerns, particularly in a period of fiscal constraint. There was certainly, and quite explicitly, a lack of enthusiasm for sales among Norwich councillors. But what was being argued was not a defiance of the law but a resistance to central attempts to determine the pattern of allocation of resources and the order of priorities. If other authorities chose to put the sales policy at the top of their priorities, as many did, that was (presumably) perfectly reasonable provided it was the outcome of local democratic processes and not the product of central dictat. What was worse was the setting of priorities by a central government which was at the same time severely limiting the resources available to meet the full range of statutory obligations. From the point of view of Ministers, Norwich were acting unreasonably and were clearly politically opposed to a policy which had a mandate at national level. Westminster was the supreme power and the sale of council houses was one of the major electoral promises of the Conservative government. The question of the conflict between national and local mandates has arisen in similar confrontations between national and local governments and will be referred to later. As an aside, however, it is of some interest that the Norwich Labour council campaigned at the municipal election of 1979 - which took place on the same day as the general election - on a policy of no council house sales and increased its majority. As Councillor Fullman remarked, "just as the government could argue that it was part of their national Manifesto, we could argue that it was part of our local Manifesto....."[34]

As agreed at the previous meeting of council, Len Stevenson, the Leader, wrote directly to Michael Heseltine reiterating the views conveyed by Tony Glover to DOE. Again the emphasis was on the council's reasonableness and its willingness to comply with the law. It also questioned whether there was any legal justification for intervention on the ground of rate of progress since this was not referred to in the Act. The tone was firm but conciliatory:

"We are writing to you, as the responsible Councillors, to say that we were surprised to learn of the views which Mr. Rumble attributed to you for we do not find in the Act any reference to a rate of progress or to a criterion of its acceptability to Ministers. We do not know what impressions you may have been given by the reports that will have been made to you but as the Leader of the Council and the Chairman of its Housing Committee we are in a position to advise you that the Council is in no way seeking to deprive the citizens it represents of their rights under the law.

However, it also appears from the general terms of Mr. Rumble's letter that you may be under some misapprehension about the steps which the City Council of Norwich is taking to comply with the Act, having regard to the other obligations laid on the Council and the resources available for this and other purposes.

We need not conceal from you our opinion that this particular piece of legislation was not well advised. Nevertheless, Parliament has thought fit to enact it and it is the firm intention of this Authority to comply with the law which Parliament has made.

In view of the misunderstandings and possible misrepresentations on this point which seem to have occurred, we are writing to request a meeting with you in order that Councillors may have the opportunity of explaining the position in Norwich to you at first hand - rather than through the intermediary of officials. We appreciate that you are a busy Minister with many pressing engagements, but for our part we shall be ready to come to London for this purpose on any date that may be convenient".[35]

On 15 September the deputation from Norwich City Council met John Stanley and officers of the DOE at Marsham Street. Those present were as follows:

Department of the Environment

Mr John Stanley	Minister of State for Housing and Construction
Mr R. J. A. Sharp	
Mr I. M. Edye	Regional Controller (Housing)
Mr N. W. Summerton	
Mr G. E. Clare	(Valuation Office Liaison Officer)
Mr R. Young	
Ms P. Griffiths	

Norwich City Council

Cllr L. Stevenson	Leader of the Council
Cllr G. Richards	Leader of the Minority Conservative Group
Cllr P. Hollis	Deputy Leader of the Council
Cllr D. Fullman	Chairman of the Housing Committee
Cllr D. Pratt	Vice Chairman, Housing Committee
Mr A. Glover	Chief Executive
Mr P. Saunders	Director of Housing and Estates
Mr P. Rosson	Assistant Director of Administration

68

Having welcomed the council's representatives, John Stanley invited them to put their case. Len Stevenson began by reiterating their concern that the Minister had an erroneous impression of recalcitrance on the part of Norwich. He emphasised the council's high reputation in service delivery, particularly in housing. But he was concerned about the "tone of the most recent letters from the Department (which) indicated that it might be felt that the council was deliberately going slow....." Tony Glover endorsed these remarks and went on to outline Norwich's substantial housing responsibilities ("half of the total housing stock in the City.....a capital value of about £500m.....waiting list stood at some 4,000") and its relative inexperience in the disposal of council houses. He was particularly concerned that the proper procedures should be observed in order to safeguard the interests of all parties:

> "the tenants wishing to buy and those not wishing to buy, and people on the waiting list. As a result of right to buy applications £20m worth of assets might be sold and the Council wished to exercise proper care in arranging the disposals".[36]

The council was, therefore, implementing the Act. A reasonable machinery had been established, the rate of progress had increased and would continue to do so. Glover added that the need for care in the disposal of dwellings had been underlined by the fact that the first sale (one of four completions) had been to a couple who already owned two houses! This had caused a certain amount of embarrassment to the council.

At this point George Richards, the leader of the Conservative group on the council, provided a rather different view of the procedures. Whilst accepting that the legislation was being implemented he felt that it was not being carried out in a method designed to accelerate progress. Rather it was more likely to hinder speedy expedition. Two particular procedures were singled out as obstructive - the practice of financial counselling prior to valuation work and the need for committee approval of valuations. Tenants who had applied were now "despairing about the slow progress of their applications".[37]

Again Pat Hollis made the point that the counselling procedures were not new but derived from problems experienced with local authority mortgages for private buyers "where some 10% of mortgagees defaulted". Stevenson responded to Richards by questioning the 'despair' among applicants when he had received only one letter from tenants complaining about lack of progress on sales but "10 to 12 letters a week from those seeking council housing". Richards remarked that prospective purchasers were unlikely to complain to Labour councillors since their opposition to sales was well publicised.

At this point Stanley interrupted this local debate and stated his position on progress:

"The rate so far, and the lack of any indication of future progress compared unfavourably with the position in other local authorities of similar size, political complexion, and inexperience in selling. For example, according to the most recent information available to the Department, Blyth Valley had issued 507 section 10 notices; Bolsover, 576; Carlisle, 672; Crawley, 810; North Tyneside, 872; Knowsley, 1,336; and Harlow, 2,614. The Council's own figures, supplied to the Department, showed that as at the end of June only 229 cases had been referred for detailed valuation out of 837 cases then admitted; at the end of July, and at the end of August, the corresponding figures were only 236 and 238 respectively. 53 valuations had been completed by the end of June; 126 by the end of July; and 130 by the end of August (an increase of only 4 over the month). 35 section 10 notices had been issued as at 20th May; 53 at the end of June (an increase of 18 in the month); 70 at the end of July (an increase of 17); and 101 at the end of August (an increase of 31). This rate of progress gave reason for tenants to feel deeply concerned. As against the one complaint received by Councillor Stevenson, the Department's Regional Office had received 54 written complaints from Norwich tenants since October 1980 - more than in any other authority in East Anglia. Further, the Council had introduced a system whereby tenants could only exchange their council homes by forfeiting their right to buy: Ministers considered this a serious breach of the spirit of the legislation, which was not consistent with the Council's stated intention not to obstruct the law, and had already announced their intention to legislate to prevent this practice".[38]

Stanley went on to ask whether the council was willing to forgo the practice of counselling and broad band valuations in order to speed up progress on the issue of Section 10 notices. Both Pat Hollis and Len Stevenson responded by stressing the helpfulness of financial counselling particularly at a time of high unemployment and redundancy. It was, they said, similar to the sort of discussion prospective purchasers had with their building society. Again Richards intervened querying the relevance on the counselling check list of a reference to the difficulty which a tenant might have in reselling the property if a Labour government returned to power. Also, he said, since in 50% of cases tenants obtained mortgage finance from a building society, a system of voluntary counselling would make it unnecessary for half the applicants.

Indeed, it was the timing rather than the existence of the counselling device which concerned Stanley and the DOE representatives. Why not offer counselling after the Section 10 offers had been made? This would speed up progress and reduce the scope to those who required a local authority mortgage. Besides, he argued, tenants had a statutory right to a mortgage "irrespective of possible default at a later stage".[39]

Discussion then focused on the rate of monthly valuations which was at the centre of the conflict. Norwich had offered a rate of 30 valuations a month which Stanley considered "incompatible with tenants being able to exercise their Right to Buy effectively and expeditiously". Again the argument was put to Norwich that the use of private valuers or the District Valuer would substantially increase this rate of processing applications. Norwich maintained that this was both costly and subject to legal difficulties given the appellate role performed by the District Valuer in the case of determinations under Section 11 of the Act. Stanley responded by illustrating the use of the District Valuer by a large number of authorities (122,000 applications referred, 94,000 completed by the end of July) and stating "that there was nothing in the statute which prevented the use of the District Valuer and a procedure had been drawn up to protect the independence of the appellate valuation".[40] If the council would consider increasing the rate of in-house valuations combined with the services of the District Valuer all outstanding Section 10 notices could be issued by the end of the year.

This was the sort of timetable that the DOE and Stanley wanted Norwich committed to. But the majority response from Norwich was that the use of the DV would result in only marginal savings in time ("only 10%.....as the District Valuer would still have to be provided with the requisite information and appropriate support") and that such a timetable would require the council to shift considerable resources away from other commitments. Moreover, as Pat Hollis reminded the Minister, the council had to be "mindful of their duties on homelessness, council house waiting lists and employment promotion".[41] And regardless of those considerations, a timetable requiring the issue of all outstanding Section 10 notices by the end of the year would involve a rather hurried disposal of £20 million worth of assets.

As the meeting drew to a close Stanley reminded them of the powers of intervention available to the Secretary of State. Such an intervention could have serious "financial implications for the Council.....and for individual councillors". This kind of statement was made on a number of occasions but in view of the subsequent judicial comment on the case probably never had real legal foundation. In view of this its repeated use could be construed as a piece of calculated intimidation. Norwich had refused to agree to a timetable and one that satisfied the Secretary of State. It was this aspect which distinguished Norwich from the other authorities which had been threatened with intervention. Other such meetings had produced firm commitments on expected progress. Greenwich who were the most likely candidates for intervention had agreed to an acceptable formula for progress at this stage. Stanley concluded by asking Norwich to consider the following points within a short time:

"whether the Council were willing to proceed with instructions for detailed valuation as soon as practicable after issuing form RTB2, without interposing the requirement for a counselling interview;

whether the Council were willing to carry out the detailed valuation without the present requirement for a broad-band valuation;

whether the Council were willing to increase their present rate of valuations from 30 per month to a higher figure: and if so, from what month that increase would take effect and what that higher figure would be;

whether the Council were willing to use the services of the District Valuer; if so, from what date referrals to the District Valuer could be expected: and at what monthly rate; and in the light of the Council's decisions on these points, and in the light of their clear statutory obligations, the Council were invited to indicate a precise date by which they would issue the balance of section 10 notices, bearing in mind the clear indications from Ministers that this should be no later than 31st December 1981".[42]

Norwich were required to respond by 25 September.

It is important to appreciate the impression made on some members of the Norwich delegation by this meeting. One member of the group was horrified at the way Stanley treated the council Leader. The Minister appeared to have already made his mind up and discussion with him was "like talking to a tank". The Leader of the council was reported as saying "The style of the meeting was something I haven't met in the 21 years I have served on the council. I haven't been treated like a naughty schoolboy as I was today. And, as Leader of the council, I must now consider whether it is worthwhile trying to run sensible local government....If central government is going to run local authorities, then central government had better get on with it. I want nothing to do with it".[43] Press reports of this meeting referred to 'an ultimatum to sell 800 council houses by the end of the year' and stated 'if it (Norwich) doesn't meet that target the Government will step in and take over the operation'.[44]

A formal letter requesting the council's response to the above points arrived the following day. On 23 September the Housing Committee met and considered the Minister's requests and a draft response. Saunders had suggested various courses of action which seemed 'reasonable'. There then followed detailed discussion of financial counselling, the valuation procedure and other areas of conflict with the Minister. A motion was put which would have satisfied the demands of the Secretary of State. It would have increased the number of cases referred to the Mortgages (Joint) Sub-Committee to 90 per month and combined with the processing of 400 applications by the DV would have achieved the target of 800 sales by the end of the year.

Such a target was, however, argued to be unrealistic and would involve unacceptable neglect of "other more important areas of housing". The motion was lost by seven votes to two. Nevertheless, Norwich moved their position on a number of issues and agreed to meet the Minister half way. The meeting agreed that:

1. financial counselling be omitted prior to the issue of the Section 10 notice but that the counselling service continue to be made available after the issue of the notices;

2. broad banding be discontinued;

3. the number of cases presented to the Mortgages (Joint) Sub-Committee be increased to 60 per month, with effect from October, 1981;

4. the Estates Surveyor be authorised to discuss with the District Valuer possible ways in which he could be of assistance to the council and that the Chairmen of this Committee and of the Mortgages (Joint) Sub-Committee be invited to attend any such meetings;

5. the Minister be informed that, at 60 cases per month, the outstanding Section 10 notices will be issued, at the latest, by October 1982 and that that date could be advanced if the Council decided to utilise the services of the District Valuer.[45]

Following that meeting a reply was sent to Stanley from Len Stevenson detailing the various amendments to procedures which the council had agreed to make. The issue of timetabling remained the sticking point. Norwich were still not committed to the use of the District Valuer but had simply agreed to "enter into discussions".[46] And the letter concluded by restating the date for the completion of outstanding valuations as October 1982 (if the District Valuer was not used). This was, of course, the target date which had already proved totally unacceptable to Ministers. Press reports referred to Norwich's actions as 'a major climb down' but saw the lack of movement on the timetable as leaving Norwich 'still on a collision course'.[47] Given that Ministers knew what rates of processing applications (especially using the DV) could be achieved such reports were certainly not ill-informed.

The response from Robin Sharp at the DOE was prompt in reiterating the unacceptability of the October 1982 date. The letter concluded "Ministers are concerned that your Councillors should be fully aware of how serious for them are the possible implications of the present position. I am therefore to ask you to provide each member of your Council with the full text of this letter for their personal attention".[48] Their personal attention was being drawn to the repeated threat of imminent intervention and potential surcharging. Two comments from senior officers of Norwich are relevant at this stage. First, it was argued that the government's insistence on a rate of sale was not accompanied by any guidelines or assistance over the sale of difficult properties. Technical and legal problems in the sale of flats were being experienced by all local authorities and DOE was better at imposing deadlines than advice over how to achieve them. Secondly, the legal officers of the council had advised members that there was no likelihood of surcharge. What was involved was a difference of opinion on the interpretation of statute and neither wilful misconduct nor actions contrary to the law.

On 14 October, Saunders outlined the developing situation to the Mortgages (Joint) Sub-Committee. Having listed the amendments to procedures already agreed by the Housing Committee, he went on to suggest that they could attempt to meet the Minister's demands by substantially increasing the rate of valuation carried out by the Estates Survey or referring applications to the District Valuer or a combination of them both. And he added:

> "Although it has not been expressly stated, the unavoidable conclusion from recent correspondence is that failure by the Council to satisfy the Minister's requirements would probably result in the Secretary of State exercising his default powers".

He then outlined the process of intervention and the financial costs which might be borne by the council. If a notice of intervention was served how should Norwich respond?

> "The Council might attempt to challenge the notice by applying in the High Court for an injunction to prevent the Secretary of State from intervening. To be successful it would be necessary to persuade the Court that tenants in Norwich were not having 'difficulty in exercising the right to buy effectively and expeditiously', and that the Secretary of State's action was therefore unreasonable".

And he continued:

> "If a notice was not challenged, or a challenge failed, the Secretary of State would assume the Council's valuation and conveyancing responsibilities for Council house sales. The consequence for the Council would be primarily financial.
>
> In addition to being deprived, albeit temporarily, of capital receipts from sales, the Council would suffer

the loss of interest on these receipts, and the costs incurred by the Secretary of State.

However, the Director of Administration is of the opinion that a very strong case could be made against the District Auditor taking any action to that effect. But one cannot be certain of the result. Certainty could only be established by challenging such a decision in the Courts".[49]

The risk, it seems, was worth taking. In order to accede to the Minister's demands additional staff would be required - five or six at a cost of £120,000. And the committee continued to take the view that the use of the DV was 'improper'. But there was a further issue of principle involved. Chairing the meeting in the absence of Fullman, Councillor Ashley remarked "it was not the intention of the council to change its priorities in order to sell council houses more quickly".[50] Whether or not Norwich would have acceded to a demand to change its priorities for a more sympathetic cause is open to question. Certainly, Norwich had expressed the nature of the disagreement all along as being about autonomy in the determination of its own local priorities and not about selling council houses. The council, said Ashley in drawing the meeting to a close "would determine its own priorities, within the law". It was thus resolved among other things, not to make use of the District Valuer. Intervention it seemed was inevitable.

A few days later Tony Glover wrote to Ian Edye at DOE attempting to defuse the situation but firmly expressing the council's resentment at being 'bullied' and misrepresented. "The Government and the City Council seem set on a collision course". The tone of the letters which Norwich had received, was, he said "peremptory". The council had not been told why it was behaving unreasonably, simply that its progress was 'totally unacceptable'. He ended, ".....I think it is important that the Department should understand how the matter is seen from here and so far the Department does not seem to understand".[51]

It was in October that Norwich first took advice on their legal position. They obtained this from Charles Cross, a former town clerk who specialised in local government and housing law. Cross advised Norwich that there would be a good chance of success in challenging a notice served under Section 23 of the Housing Act.

76

City brand Minister 'unreasonable'

HESELTINE URGED 'GET OFF BACKS OF COUNCIL'

Housing: Norwich council rebels

Such action would have to be taken quickly and Norwich decided to retain Cross's advice.

The Secretary of State

On 29 October Len Stevenson received a letter from Michael Heseltine. This stressed the extreme seriousness of the situation and the fact that Norwich stood out among all the authorities which had received a formal warning as being the one with the worst timetable on the issue of Section 10 notices. Contingency arrangements had therefore been set in hand in connection with the use of the powers under Section 23:

> "However, before reaching a decision and in view of the extremely serious financial consequences intervention could have for the Council's ratepayers and in certain circumstances for members of the Council in their personal capacities, I wish to give your Council one further opportunity to reconsider its timetable".[52]

For this purpose a final meeting was proposed. The meeting was arranged for 5 November. The agenda was apparently leaked to the press before the date was known to Stevenson. The Guardian contacted him saying that they had been briefed by the DOE that the meeting was intended "to give the Council one last chance before the Minister brought in the lawyers". Stevenson subsequently wrote to Heseltine's Private Secretary describing such action as "extremely discourteous" and pointing out that "the Press seemingly, are better informed than the Council is about the Council's business".[53] It may be that DOE was already sensitising the press to the inevitable outcome. From previous meetings and correspondence it was clear that unless Norwich was willing to accept, and implement, policies to meet an end of December deadline for the issue of outstanding offers then the outcome of intervention was inevitable. Norwich had by now considered and rejected the use of the DV (more work, more expense) and their target date of October 1982 remained. It was unlikely that the gap of eight months would be bridged at this meeting.

Certainly, those attending from Norwich took the view that decisions had already been made and this was a mere rubber stamping operation. Describing his perception of the meeting with Heseltine, one councillor recalls:

> "My Vice Chairman didn't turn up to that meeting because, having been at the Stanley meeting where we

were harangued as though we were a group of recalcitrant schoolchildren he said that it would be a waste of his time and blood pressure to turn up. In fact, I got the impression that it was a waste of all of our time. At the time he (Heseltine) had just been censured by the courts for withdrawing grant without consultation from Camden and we all got the impression that the only reason why Heseltine wheeled us in and saw us was that he didn't want to be criticised in the courts again for riding roughshod when he did send the commissioner and the only thing that we were in any doubt of was the date when the commissioner would be sent in when we came out of the meeting".[54]

The apparent significance of this meeting was evident from the involvement of not only Michael Heseltine himself, but the two Members of Parliament for Norwich, John Garrett and David Ennals, both Labour.*

Meeting with the Secretary of State for the Environment, Department of the Environment, Marsham Street, London Thursday, 5 November, 1981

Representing the City Council

    Councillor D. Fullman
    Councillor P. Hollis
    Councillor P. Mercer
    Councillor P. Moore
    Councillor L. A. Stevenson

    Rt Hon David Ennals, MP
    John Garrett, MP

A. R. H. Glover	Chief Executive Officer
P. Saunders	Director of Housing and Estates
P. Rosson	Assistant Director of Administration

---

*It is worth noting that at the 1979 General Election both of the Norwich constituencies returned Labour MPs. Previously one party had failed to win both seats.

Rt Hon Michael Heseltine, MP   Secretary of State
for the Environment

John Stanley MP   Minister of State for
Housing and
Construction

R.J. Sharp and other officials of the Department

The Secretary of State, Michael Heseltine began the meeting by stating that Norwich had had every possible opportunity to change its position. After six months of meetings and correspondence progress to date and indication of further progress remained totally unacceptable.

There were two key issues to which he wished to hear the council's response. The date by which the balance of 693 offer letters would be issued, on the basis that October 1982 was unacceptable. He reminded the council's representatives that the services of the District Valuer were still available and he asked whether the financial consequences of intervention under Section 23 had been explained to all members of the council.

Len Stevenson replied by emphasising that Norwich had not been intransigent but had abandoned broad banding valuations, rescheduled financial counselling and in fact had doubled the rate of progress on valuations. Moreover, they were now achieving a faster rate of progress than they had originally expected. It was quite possible that they would deal with outstanding applications before October 1982. Indeed, both Len Stevenson and Pat Hollis suggested that June was a possible target date. This would, however, involve omitting a certain number of 'difficult' properties such as flats and maisonettes.

There was then some discussion of exact numbers involved. John Stanley, at one point, queried the discrepancy between a figure of 491 and 450 outstanding applications. On the face of it this seems an extraordinary level of detail to involve two senior members of the government and difficult to imagine in other areas of housing policy. Debates at that level usually concern discrepancies of millions of pounds rather than tens of properties.

Heseltine's general tone was firm and threatening although more courteous than Stanley's had been. Had members of the council, he asked, "been informed of the financial consequences of intervention"? Were they aware of the "personal consequences"? Were they aware of "his power to retain capital receipts and mortgage payments....that he was not liable to account for interest....that the loss of revenue from sales would have block grant implications"?[55]

He refused to be drawn on exactly what he meant by 'personal consequences' for members. And given the particular circumstances of the conflict this was indeed always an unlikely outcome.

The issue of the role of the District Valuer was again discussed, with Councillor Mercer commenting that "refusal to use its services was the biggest single obstacle to increasing the rate of progress".[56] But Norwich refused to shift its position on this, reiterating the marginal savings in time involved and the complicating factor of his appellate role. This produced the, by now, ritual and accurate observation from Stanley that this was not a problem which appeared to trouble a large number of other authorities who had made extensive use of the District Valuer.

Whilst much of the meeting went over the same ground as the earlier meeting with Stanley there was some movement on both sides. Norwich predicted but did not promise increased progress (possibly a June deadline). Stanley for his part suggested that a reasonable schedule would aim for a mid-February deadline. The gap had now narrowed to just over three months. Councillor Moore remarked that a disagreement over three months "seemed to be a small gap to give rise to considering taking such a severe step".[57]

Norwich MPs and councillors maintained their position that a number of steps had been taken to comply with the wishes of DOE and they were being perfectly reasonable in the circumstances. But as Heseltine remarked "it was also necessary....to take into account tenants and other local authorities. The council's rate of progress was not comparable to others...." It was his responsibility "to achieve the objectives of the Act...." Indeed it emerged that comparability with other authorities was not the issue. "Norwich", said Heseltine, "was a case on its own".[58] This seemed to refer to the number of complaints which had been received from Norwich tenants rather than comparable performance. Other authorities may have been similarly guilty on this score but they had agreed to acceptable deadlines. On the question of complaints, both David Ennals and John Garrett commented that "they had received no complaints from any of their constituents alleging delay over house sales".[59]

It was apparent that the only means of escape for Norwich was to agree to the use of the District Valuer. But Norwich had moved as far as they were prepared to go. They had agreed to discuss the matter with the District Valuer. Those discussions had taken place and had simply confirmed the reservations which Norwich had. The District Valuer in Norwich, said Fullman "took the matter very seriously and would be involved in each initial valuation". This reinforced the council's fears that his valuation and appellate function could not be separated.

As the meeting drew to a conclusion Pat Hollis suggested a further meeting in mid-January to assess progress. Heseltine was not prepared to accept this. Whilst not denying that Norwich had its own priorities to consider he "had his own responsibilities and duties which included powers of intervention". Councillor Mercer observed that "the Council was now using meetings with Ministers as a method of delay".[60]

Len Stevenson summed up the general feelings of the Norwich representatives - "While the Council had made concessions, the Secretary of State had not moved his position at all....if intervention did follow he would have no hesitation in advising the Council to challenge such action in the Courts".[61] Heseltine required a reply to his earlier suggestions by Friday 13 November.

Returning to Norwich there was little doubt in the minds of the Norwich party that intervention was inevitable and imminent:

> "We did discuss whether or not to make a last ditch offer. Not that we would meet their timetable because by that stage it was impossible, but that we would actually try to cut the time between when we felt that we could clear the backlog and when the backlog was wanting to be cleared by the DOE, cut the four months down. It was decided that that would really be a waste of time because it was quite obvious that they'd made their minds up and the only way to get us off the hook would have been to complete by February which was impossible anyway. We warned Heseltine at the time that we would actually go through the courts and challenge his rights, etc. He seemed to enjoy that".[62]

The next day a letter arrived from Sharp at the DOE which conveyed Heseltine's concern "that there might still be misunderstandings about the help which the District Valuer could give to the council...." There then followed a fairly detailed account of the procedures involved and the sort of information required by the District Valuer. The general thrust was that whilst the District Valuer and his Deputy would be involved initially in each valuation in order to ensure that adequate information was available on the general levels of valuation in the city they would not undertake work on Section 10 notices on individual dwellings. Thus, if later called to make a determination under Section 11 the appellate function would not be compromised. Contrary to Fullman's account, Sharp stated that "the District Valuer in Norwich has confided to us that this was the position he was seeking to explain at the meeting he had with the Chairman of Housing Committee".[63] There were apparently standing instructions designed to preserve the appellate role of the District Valuer in this context. The second part of the letter argued that the information required by the District Valuer was both simpler to provide and less extensive than Norwich claimed.

On 10 November there was a public meeting of the General Purposes Committee of the council which considered a full and detailed report by Tony Glover, the Chief Executive Officer. The report began by summarising the factual position on progress at 6 November. Just over 900 applications to buy had been accepted and 251 formal offers had been issued. He continued:

> "To sum up so far: the Council is at present forecasting completion by September for all cases; or completion by June for cases except difficult cases. These are forecasts: they are not commitments agreed with Ministers. By contrast, Ministers propose a February completion date for all cases, including difficult ones. This, they say, is consistent with a target which is being achieved in other authorities, perhaps with the aid of the District Valuer or use of the private sector. Intervention under Section 23 is threatened if the Council does not agree this target".[64]

Glover then outlined four different grounds for complying with these Ministerial requests.

1. because that is what the law requires;
2. because it is what Ministers are asking;
3. because it would be to the council's financial advantage;

4.   because otherwise there will be intervention under Section 23; and this will have adverse financial consequences for the council (and ratepayers) and, possibly, for members.[65]

On the legal question he emphasised the phrase in the Act "effectively and expeditiously":

"There is no definition in the Act of 'effectively and expeditiously'. The question to be asked, therefore - and this is presumably how the courts would look at the matter - is something like 'Is what the Council is doing reasonable? Would a reasonable man say that the tenants of the City Council are able to exercise the right to buy effectively and expeditiously?' It is a question of judgement.

Ministers say that other authorities are achieving a faster rate of progress than this. But the Council is not responsible for circumstances in other places than Norwich, and Counsel has advised that Ministers would not be able to draw comparisons with other authorities if it came to testing the matter in the courts. Ministers also say that there have been many complaints from Norwich tenants, in fact a greater number than from tenants of any other authority in Norfolk. I do not know how recent these complaints are; if there are many recent complaints, that would be an indication that the right is not exercisable effectively and expeditiously. Norwich MPs say they have received no complaints.

This is the fundamental question: are tenants able to exercise the right to buy effectively and expeditiously? It is a question for the judgement of members".[66]

Should Norwich agree simply because this was what Ministers were asking? Glover's observations on this pointed to the breaking from tradition on the part of Ministers rather than any change in practice or stance by Norwich:

"The practice of Local Government in this country depends on co-operation between local and central government. On the traditional model, Ministers make requests to local authorities which are on the whole reasonable, and local authorities on the whole comply with them - to a degree, and on a timescale, which will vary from place to place because circumstances differ from one place to another. Most unfortunately, this traditional ethic is breaking down (and not only over this question of council house sales).

Ministers are not taking their stand on the traditional ground. They are saying that what the Council is doing is "totally unacceptable" and that what they want done must be done because otherwise there will be intervention under Section 23".[67]

In dealing with the financial implication to the council of the speed of implementation (leaving aside the costs which might be incurred through intervention under Section 23) Glover discussed the pros and cons of early capital receipts versus the cost of resources required to speed up valuations. A detailed document had been prepared which, in fact, suggested that an accelerated sales programme would provide a net benefit to the Housing Revenue Account of only £249,000 as opposed to £308,000 working to a target date of June 1982. He concluded that:

"These financial considerations are important. They are elements - not the only ones - in the judgement the Council makes about whether it is implementing the Act reasonably. There is not a strong and clear argument, in financial terms, for moving at this speed rather than that".[68]

He then came to perhaps the most significant part of his report regarding the possible action to be taken by Norwich and the consequences in relation to intervention under Section 23. The council had said that it was prepared to take court action if such a notice was served. His advice was that:

"It will not be in the best interests of the Council, or of members in their personal capacities, to allow a Section 23 notice to be issued and run its course unchallenged".

The general reasons for this advice were that:

"If an action were joined in the courts, neither side could be certain of the outcome. The ground of the Council's case would be that it was acting reasonably, and that the Secretary of State was using his very great powers unreasonably. Counsel advises that the Council would have a reasonable prospect of success: more important, that the court would be bound to hear the matter.

It seems to me that if the Council were to take action in the courts and lose, it would not be in a worse position than it now is, apart from the expense of the action. The action would take time, and by the time it had been concluded the valuations might all have been settled (assuming that they continued to be processed while the court action was proceeding). If it lost, the Council would do whatever the court ordered as regards the outstanding cases".[69]

Glover went on to deal with more specific consequences of intervention. The financial penalties would indeed be "substantial" but difficult to quantify. If a Section 23 notice became operative the administrative consequences would be "conflict, uncertainty and confusion". There would be two sources of power and authority operating in the Town Hall. In relation to the political consequences for individual members he advised:

"The Director of Administration is of the opinion that, although losses would certainly be incurred by the Council if there were intervention under Section 23, those losses would be attributable not to wilful misconduct, but to a difference of opinion between the Council and Central Government as to how the Act should be implemented. I agree with that opinion".

Glover's principal conclusion from these various considerations was that:

"I have emphasised at several points in this report that in my opinion the basic question is whether tenants of the Council are able to exercise the right to buy effectively and expeditiously, and whether the Council is taking reasonable steps to enable them to do so. It follows that in my opinion the Secretary of State, in concentrating instead on the consequences that would follow from his intervention under Section 23, is directing attention to the wrong issue".[70]

Following consideration of this report, Councillor Mercer proposed a series of amendments designed to meet the mid-February deadline. These were easily defeated. A further amendment by

Councillor Mercer urging the use of the District Valuer was similarly defeated. By a large majority the meeting resolved to reaffirm the June 1982 deadline and that:

"in the event of notice being received from the Secretary of State for the Environment of his intention to exercise his powers under Section 23 of the Housing Act, 1980, and with a view to the exercise of those powers being challenged, the Director of Administration, after consultation with Councillors L. A. Stevenson, Hollis, Fullman and Pratt, be authorised to institute proceedings in the High Court by way of an Application for Judicial Review under Order 53 of the Rules of the Supreme Court and to take all necessary steps in connection therewith".[71]

The next day Len Stevenson conveyed the council's response to Michael Heseltine. He reiterated the argument about the use of the District Valuer and meeting the deadline but made more general comments regarding the priorities of Norwich in serving the needs of the locality and the changing relationship between central and local government:

"It simply will not do, in our judgement, to neglect the problems of the homeless, and other statutory housing obligations - and the work we are doing to create employment - and combat other problems - just to enable a relatively small number of people, who are already comfortably housed, to buy a property a few months earlier than they otherwise could, when they will lose nothing by waiting....For myself, I do not see how local government in this country (and I have been a Councillor for 20 years) can continue except on the basis of co-operation between central and local government - within a tradition in which the Secretary of State makes reasonable requests and a local authority makes a reasonable fist at complying with them - to a degree, and on a timescale, which may be different from that of the authority next door whose circumstances are different. But Ministers, in this case, have chosen not to stand on this traditional ground".[72]

It is perhaps additionally worth noting that two days earlier Norwich had finally received a judgement on their longstanding claim for exemption from the Right to Buy for ground floor flats.

The first application for exemption had been made in November 1980, eight months earlier. Since then Norwich had submitted a stream of applications for such exemptions. Again it seemed that local considerations had lost out. Such an exemption would only be granted if the dwelling was designed or specially adapted for occupation by persons of pensionable age <u>and</u> it is the practice of the landlord to let it only for occupation by such persons. The dwellings for which Norwich had sought exemption did not meet those criteria. Given the time it had taken DOE to come to this conclusion it seems as well that it was not central government who were in the business of processing Right to Buy applications. In a note to the Mortgages (Joint) Sub-Committee, Saunders expressed his view on the matter:

> "Although a considerable volume of correspondence has passed between the Department and the Council in this connection - the first application being submitted on 10 November 1980 with an average eight months elapsing before a decision is communicated, and notwithstanding the considerable supporting evidence put forward concerning the chronic shortage in this area of housing need - the Secretary of State has in all cases declined to make the necessary determinations which would exempt these properties from the right to buy provisions of the Act".[73]

It should be added that Norwich were by no means exceptional in being refused exemptions on these grounds - although the number of exemptions they sought were probably unusually high. In fact, by March 1982, 1,682 exemptions had been applied for by local authorities in England. Only 57 had been successful - a 3% success rate.

On 3 December, Michael Heseltine replied to Len Stevenson's letter. In this he repeated his view that tenants were being subjected to unacceptable delays. He referred to the complaints which had been received by DOE since the previous February. These complaints went beyond the question of the delay in the issue of formal offers. Heseltine referred to various aspects of the council's behaviour which could be construed as obstructive and delaying. "Reference is made in particular cases to abnormally high valuations and to unreasonable covenants. Tenants have complained about delays after service of Section 10 notices in completing sales, with particular reference in certain cases to the adverse effect of delays on their mortgage prospects...."

The reasons given for intervention therefore were broader than a disagreement over the precise timetabling of the issue of formal offers. It was presented much more as a general climate of unreasonableness on the part of Norwich. Perhaps with the court in mind it was presented as a catalogue of delaying tactics and obstructive manoeuvres.

Heseltine's letter ended:

"Having considered the matter most carefully it appears to me, whether I have regard to Norwich City Council alone or to Norwich in comparison with other authorities, that your Council's secure tenants have or may have difficulty in exercising the right to buy effectively and expeditiously and I have therefore decided to use my powers of intervention under that section. A notice of intervention is being sent to your Council today".[74]

5
CONFRONTATION AND DEFEAT

The general feeling after the meeting with Heseltine on 5 November was of a certain inevitability in the outcome. The order under Section 23 would come. It was just a question of when. After Stevenson conveyed the council's view to Heseltine on 11 November there was what one officer described as "a surprising interval of time" before anything happened. Some of the officers and members had the feeling that the Secretary of State was agonising over what might be quite a difficult political decision. After all, defeat in the courts would have substantially weakened his position in relation to other authorities on the black list, to say nothing of his position in cabinet. The Right to Buy was the principal plank of the Conservatives' housing policy and defeat in the courts could have seriously restricted its progress nationally and have been highly embarrassing. "Can you imagine if they [the judiciary] had found in favour of Norwich on any of these issues?.....Nationwide every local authority in the country would be putting two fingers up".[1]

The belief, however, that there might be further room for negotiation was ill-founded. There may have been some agonising on the part of Heseltine, Stanley and their DOE advisers but the order under Section 23 eventually arrived.

David Ennals contacted Tony Glover on the afternoon of Thursday, 3 December to tell him that a statement had been made in the House of Commons to that effect. Although relatively surprised by the decision Norwich was not unprepared. But they had to move quickly. The first step was to seek an injunction to stop the Secretary of State proceeding and an application for leave to apply for judicial review. This form of legal action requires a very tight timetable. On Friday 4, the notice of intervention arrived. By this time Norwich had contacted their counsel, Charles Cross again. On his advice, they had brought in Nigel Macleod,QC.

An application for leave to apply for judicial review had to be before Justice Glidewell by Monday 7. The officers in Norwich, with the aid of two typists, worked through Saturday to produce a detailed affidavit. The same day an advertisement in the local press announced that the Secretary of State's office would be open for business on the Monday morning. The advert in the 'Eastern Daily Press' was addressed to 'Tenants of Norwich City Council' and referred to a special temporary office providing information, and advised those on the point of serving any notice in connection with the Right to Buy to do so and send a copy to the Norwich Office of the DOE. A Norwich solicitor would handle sales and the DOE press office indicated that while no formal agreement had been reached the firm was likely to be Mills and Reeve. No reason as to why they had been selected was given but their premises were next door to those of the DOE temporary office.

Justice Glidewell granted leave for Norwich to apply for judicial review. Whilst the office of the Secretary of State did open and remained so, its presence was superfluous once the application had been granted. The seven-strong team initially brought in was reported as likely to be reduced. It should be noted that the DOE was willing to leave the administration of the Right to Buy in the hands of Norwich pending the resolution of the litigation. The press reported Justice Glidewell's decisions as a victory for Norwich. Norwich had established an 'arguable case' but while this initial victory was significant the major engagements were still to come.

The timetable for judicial review remained very tight. A detailed application had to be lodged by 1pm on Wednesday, 9 December. Again the officers in Norwich had to work into the early hours of that day to complete the necessary work. A committee room was knee deep in paperwork - Minutes of Meetings, correspondence between DOE and Norwich etc.

The affidavit was sworn before a local solicitor at 7 am on the Wednesday morning and taken on the 8.30 am train to London. One set of papers alone was 338 pages long. Indeed in examining the documentary evidence that was presented in court it is striking how exposed and accessible are the decision making processes of the local authority compared to the relative secrecy of central government. The DOE response to the Norwich affidavit was required by 5 pm on the Friday of that week. They were to be heard in the Divisional Court before Lord Justice Donaldson and Justice Goff on 17 December.

COUNCIL HOUSE SALES - THE RIGHT TO BUY

Tenants Of
Norwich City Council

A special temporary office has been set up by the Department of the Environment at Clement Court, Redwell Street, Norwich NR2 4SW. Tenants of the City Council who are in process of buying their homes and any others who wish to do so may contact this office for information. A further announcement will be made in due course.

IMPORTANT NOTE: If you are on the point of serving any notice or other document concerning the right to buy on Norwich City Council, you are advised in your own interest to serve it on the Council as soon as possible and to send a copy to the Department of the Environment at the above address.

Issued by:
The Department of the Environment,
Norwich Office,
Clement Court, Redwell Street,
Norwich NR2 4SW.
Telephone No: Norwich 612522/3/4/5

92

The case for the Secretary of State

Reflecting the letter sent by Heseltine justifying the issue of the Section 23 notice, the case made for intervention went wider than a simple disagreement over a timetable for formal offers and the use or non-use of the District Valuer. It conveyed a general climate of obstructiveness and localist petulance. It fell under five headings:

1.   Complaints from tenants

Evidence brought before the court included copies of letters of complaint from fifty tenants. They complained of delay and, in particular, delay between the time when their Right to Buy was admitted and the issue of a formal offer stating the terms and the price. The delay, claimed the Secretary of State, was currently running at 12 months. Tenants complained that this delay meant that they continued to pay rent over a lengthy period when they could have been paying off the debt on their mortgage. It was argued that such considerations were particularly relevant to more elderly tenants.

Tenants had also complained of the council's financial counselling interviews. As illustrated in earlier chapters these complaints were that counselling was an unnecessary source of delay and that certain anti-sales messages were conveyed to applicants. Thus, although the council had finally agreed to amend its procedure after the meeting with Stanley in September, its perceived deterrent aim was still an issue.

2.   Overpricing by the council

The court was provided with a detailed analysis of Norwich valuations against the determinations on appeal by the District Valuer. These illustrated, according to the Secretary of State, consistent overvaluing (and thus overpricing) and another tactic for delaying applications. In the analysis of 108 such cases, in every one a reduction had been made by the District Valuer varying from 2.3% to 24.8%. On a comparable basis it was shown that 417 offers had been made by South Norfolk, an adjoining district, with only 14 cases going to appeal. Moreover, in nine out of the 14 the District Valuer had agreed with the council's valuation.

3.   Onerous covenants

It was claimed that Norwich had chosen to impose onerous and unusual covenants upon claimants of the Right to Buy. The

Secretary of State had taken exception to two covenants in particular. Conditions 2 and 11 read as follows:

(2) "Not to erect or build or permit to be erected or built on the property any building erections or structures other than those already standing thereon at the date hereof nor to make or permit to be made any alteration or addition thereto without the written consent of the Council and then in accordance with plans sections elevations and specifications previously submitted to and approved by the Council and properly constructed to the satisfaction of the Council".

(11) "To permit the Council and its duly authorised agents with or without tools or appliances at all reasonable times to enter upon the property to view the state and condition of the same and to allow the Council to remove and dispose of any buildings or erections or other things which may be placed upon the property contrary to the stipulations herein contained and for this purpose to break and remove fences and re-enter upon the property or any part thereof upon which a breach of the foregoing stipulations may occur the Council not being responsible for anything so removed or for the loss thereof or for any damage thereto or any part of the property and to pay to the Council the costs of so doing within twenty-one days of a written demand in that behalf".

It was claimed that those conditions were not merely onerous - "they substantially limit the extent of the purchaser's right to enjoy his freehold estate". The affidavit went on to point out that the inclusion of such covenants in the Section 10 notices gave rise to delay even when the covenants were withdrawn.

4. Comparisons between the performance of Norwich City Council and other councils

Considerable statistical information had been provided comparing the performance of Norwich with other councils in implementing the Right to Buy. These data, claimed the affidavit, showed Norwich to have "one of the worst rates of progress of all the councils...." Moreover, it was claimed that several authorities had had to process a much larger number of applications. It was emphasised that while such comparisons had drawn the Secretary of State's attention to Norwich his decision to intervene was "upon the basis of the other considerations appearing upon [the] affidavit quite independently of.....comparisons". It was the rate of issue of Section 10 notices which was the main basis for comparisons and, more importantly, the failure of Norwich to agree to an acceptable timetable. It was argued that in all but a few cases an acceptable timetable had been agreed (or was likely to be agreed). Of all the authorities under scrutiny by DOE only five had issued a smaller number of Section 10 notices than Norwich at the end of October 1981. Details of these have been provided earlier in this book (Chapter 2). These were Tower Hamlets, Islington, Chester-le-Street, Watford and Copeland. In the case of Tower Hamlets, negotiations about a revised timetable were in progress and the Secretary of State indicated how seriously he viewed the position. Islington had indicated that they could now meet the timetable previously given and had received a formal warning and been invited to a Ministerial meeting. Chester-le-Street had undertaken to issue 630 notices by 31 January 1982, a timetable which was acceptable. Watford, following a formal warning letter sent at the end of July had undertaken to issue 1,265 notices by 31 December, 1981 and the formal warning had been withdrawn. Copeland were currently in discussion with DOE regarding a revised timetable.

There were, in addition to these five authorities with worse numerical performance, four others with whom progress had been taken up. Expressed as a percentage of admitted claims their performance on the issue of Section 10 notices was worse or no better than that of Norwich. Two had already agreed to satisfactory timetables.

On expected future progress the target date of June 1982 suggested by Norwich for the issue of outstanding Section 10 notices was, with the exception of Greenwich, the slowest predicted rate of progress making allowance for the number of applications involved. The conclusion offered was that the rate of progress achieved by other authorities demonstrated that the expeditious issue of outstanding offers was "a matter of will, not a matter of absolute capacity".

5.   Exchange of homes

The policy adopted by Norwich in relation to dwelling exchanges was offered as another example of the council's general attitude towards the Right to Buy legislation. Concerned about evidence which suggested 'key money' changing hands among tenants in order for mutually desirable reshuffling to occur, Norwich had decided that exchanges should be achieved by assignment and not by the grant of a new tenancy. Under Section 37 of the 1980 Act the legal consequence was the **loss** of secure tenant status. This having been achieved, all rights were then restored by "administrative action" with the exception of the Right to Buy.

6.   The use of the District Valuer

This was presented as a separate issue of disagreement and not as a ground entitling intervention. Indeed, the Secretary of State, in his submission stated:

> "It is for the Council to decide how to achieve the
> expeditious sale of Council homes and for the Secretary
> of State to consider whether that result is being
> achieved".

The affidavit then went on to detail the various grounds for disagreement in the use of the District Valuer between DOE and Norwich. These have been discussed at some length in earlier sections. The general point made to the court was that the objection made by Norwich lacked any substance and that 250 other local authorities had made use of the District Valuer without any apparent difficulties.

The attitude towards the use of the District Valuer combined with the other objections referred to above demonstrated, claimed the affidavit, that Norwich had "neglected opportunities to deal effectively and expeditiously with the right to buy and that it (had) from the first sought to inhibit and postpone the due process of tenants' claims under the Act...."

The case for Norwich

Responding to these claims Nigel Macleod, acting for Norwich, attacked the decision to intervene under Section 23 on six grounds. Firstly he claimed, citing the case of **Assoc Prov Picture Houses Ltd versus Wednesbury Corporation (1948),** it is unreasonable for the Secretary of State to intervene unless the council has acted unreasonably because the words "exercising the right to buy effectively and expeditiously" in Section 23 must be linked with the words "as soon as practicable" in Section 10 of the Act. He went on to argue that "the intervention must be related to the discharge of the statutory function and to the statutory obligation". The council had discharged its statutory obligation in implementing the Right to Buy. The issue of Section 10 notices, however, was a step which had to be taken "as soon as practicable". The evidence, claimed Macleod, showed that the council had not acted unreasonably in relation to the issue of Section 10 notices.

Secondly, the Secretary of State had acted unreasonably in failing to take into account the council's overall duties, other than the Right to Buy.

Thirdly, Macleod rehearsed the objections put forward by Norwich on numerous occasions on the use of the District Valuer in the preparation of Section 10 notices. "It would be unlawful to use the District Valuer for these purposes because of the appellate or arbitration duties of the District Valuer under Section 11...."

Fourthly, the Secretary of State had acted unreasonably because he had justified his intervention in part on matters which he had never taken up with the authority; namely onerous covenants; improper valuation bases; over-high valuations.

Fifthly, he had acted unreasonably in taking into account comparable performances. Circumstances varied from one authority to another.

Finally, argued Macleod, he had acted unreasonably in operating these powers when there was only three and a half months difference between what the Minister and what the council thought could reasonably be achieved. This was particularly unreasonable given the council's improved performance in the issue of Section 10 notices.

The judgement

In delivering his judgement, Donaldson LJ began by outlining the role of the court and the powers of the Secretary of State in this case. The Right to Buy, he said "was and is politically controversial. So is the decision of the Secretary of State to intervene in the case of houses owned by the Norwich City Council". In such circumstances he suggested "the role of the court and the nature of its decisions are liable to be misunderstood". But the court "is deaf to all political considerations. It is not concerned with whether the Secretary of State was wise or unwise to intervene. Its sole concern is to do its duty of inquiring whether the Secretary of State had power to intervene. If he had no such power, his action is an abuse of power and this court will protect the Norwich City Council by setting aside his decision. If he had the power to intervene, the court will stand aside and it will be for Parliament to judge whether or not he should have done so".

He then reminded the court of the phrasing of Section 23 of the Housing Act, 1980. He stressed in particular that the Secretary of State had powers to intervene "if it appears to him" that tenants are experiencing difficulty in exercising their Right to Buy "effectively and expeditiously". It was of no consequence if it did not appear so to the court, to Norwich City Council "or to anyone else that exists". The test, he said, is "basically subjective".

The Secretary of State's assertion that a certain state of affairs existed could be challenged if the court was satisfied that the assertion was untruthful or that he was "acting otherwise than in good faith". It could be challenged if he had not explained "why the relevant circumstances appeared to him to exist". Donaldson referred to **Secretary of State for Employment v ASLEF No 2 (1972)** where such a judgement had been made. In the Norwich case, however, the reason for the intervention had been explained. Whilst these reasons could be examined the issue was not whether the court would have reached the same conclusion. The question was whether the reasons are such that "the Secretary of State could properly reach the conclusion which he has reached". In other words, was it a reasonable conclusion to reach given the evidence before the court?

He then reviewed the arguments put before the court by the Secretary of State and Norwich. Having done so he proceeded to dismiss the various submissions put forward by Nigel Macleod. In his first two submissions, Macleod had argued that Norwich was fulfilling its statutory duties, was acting reasonably and issuing section notices as soon as was practicable. These considerations were, according to Donaldson, irrelevant because they ignored the wording of Section 23. There was no suggestion that Norwich was defying the law. "At most all that is said is that the Council shows a marked lack of enthusiasm for the legislation, amounting perhaps to distaste". Without doubt, he said, the council has many statutory duties and it has a discretion and a duty to decide priorities. It can reasonably decide to give sales a low priority but the consequence may be that tenants experience difficulty in exercising their Right to Buy. If so, it may become justified for the Secretary of State to intervene.

Thus, the wording of Section 23 was such that a judgement that Norwich was acting reasonably was consistent with a judgement that circumstances had arisen that justified intervention on the part of the Secretary of State. The question was whether it could have reasonably <u>appeared</u> to the Secretary of State that tenants were experiencing difficulties regardless of the reasonableness of Norwich. All the evidence mobilised to demonstrate that Norwich City Council were doing a reasonable job on selling council houses given their other duties, statutory and otherwise, was of little relevance.

Macleod's second submission was that Section 23 was a "penal power" and as such only exercisable if the authority is in breach of its statutory duty. Donaldson disagreed with its description as a penal power arguing that there were no necessarily serious financial consequences and added that surcharging of individual councillors was an unlikely outcome since the intervention was not a response to a breach of statutory duty. Heseltine's earlier threats regarding the "personal consequences" for members seemed, therefore, to have had little legal substance.

Turning to the use of the District Valuer, Donaldson repeated the arguments against the Norwich position. There was no question, he said, of there being a "duty" on the part of the council to use the services of the District Valuer. All that was being said was that it <u>appeared</u> to the Secretary of State that difficulties were being experienced by tenants in exercising their Right to Buy. "In so far as this is due to staff shortages the problem could be relieved by using the District Valuer, private valuer or by taking on temporary staff". What are the objections? Norwich insist on using 1/500 plans. The Secretary of State has pointed out that other authorities do not use them. There is an 'ethical objection' because of the appellate function of the District Valuer. But special arrangements have been made. "In this context he (the Secretary of State) was influenced by the fact that 250 other local authorities appear to agree with him".

Donaldson went on to suggest that those special arrangements could be supplemented by a Section 10 notice having a clause in bold print

> "to the effect that if the house has been inspected by a
> valuer from the District Valuer's office, (a) the price
> and value stated are those considered appropriate by
> the landlords and do not necessarily reflect any advice

by the valuer, and (b) any determination under section 11 will be undertaken by a different and independent valuer".

This, he said, would remove Macleod's objection that

> "whilst the special arrangements might remove any injustice, the appearance of injustice remained. The tenant who knew that the house had been inspected by a District Valuer, might think, wrongly, that the section 10 notice reflected that valuer's view as to the proper price, or that any right of appeal under section 11 would be illusory since he would be appealing to the person or office which had made the offending valuation".

But, once again, these considerations as to the rights and wrongs of using the District Valuer were of little relevance to the case. Even if Norwich were correct in their various objections that did not undermine the case for intervention under Section 23. Whatever the causes or the possible remedies open to Norwich there was an admission that "staff shortages were causing delay in the issue of Section 10 notices (and) to this extent at least it appeared to the Secretary of State that tenants were having difficulty in exercising their Right to Buy effectively or expeditiously".

Had the council been given adequate opportunity of commenting upon Heseltine's conclusion that they were "imposing unnecessarily onerous covenants, valuing upon an improper basis and over-valuing"?

Donaldson's response to that was:

> "The matters mentioned by the Secretary of State [onerous covenants and overpricing] are matters which he sees as being the cause of the tenants' difficulties, but his primary, and possibly his sole concern is with the fact of these difficulties, and it was this which was referred to the Council for comment on frequent occasions".

And on the question of comparable performance and the argument put by Macleod that such comparisons are unjustified because local circumstances vary substantially, Donaldson was equally unimpressed.

"If the Secretary of State finds that Norwich City Council is making slower progress with the process of allowing its tenants to buy their homes than most other Councils, in the absence of some explanation, which has not been forthcoming, it is difficult to see why he has erred in taking this into account when concluding that tenants of the City Council are in fact experiencing difficulty in exercising the right to buy".

Finally, there was the submission that the use of such power was unjustified given that the various negotiations between the Ministers and Norwich produced in the end a disagreement amounting to three and a half months between the timetable demanded and the timetable offered. Again the wording of Section 23 circumvented such an objection. "I repeat that we are not concerned with whether it is or is not reasonable to intervene: only with whether the power to intervene has arisen". But he added that "three and a half months on top of the period which has already elapsed for tenants seeking to buy is a long time".

In drawing the proceedings to a close he again pointed out that it was not for the court to consider - "still less to express a view on" - whether it would have reached the same conclusion as the Secretary of State. The testimony given by him was _true_ and _bona fide_; he had not taken account of immaterial matters or failed to take account of material ones; he had not misdirected himself in law. "On the evidence it is quite impossible to say that the conclusions reached by the Secretary of State is one which was not open to him". The application was dismissed with costs.

Norwich members had already given permission to take the case to the Court of Appeal should this prove necessary. This was the immediate decision following the failure in the Divisional Court. Both Cross and Macleod advised Norwich that there was ample scope for appeal. Nevertheless there was some surprise at their swift dismissal in the Divisional Court. As one of the legal officers remarked "we went down with a dull thud". Donaldson had clearly been distinctly unimpressed by the case put by Norwich. There was a feeling in the Norwich camp that the arguments they had propounded had not been analysed properly. There was some suspicion that the approach taken by Donaldson and Goff reflected their experience as commercial lawyers. It "seemed to us that the approach to the case was in terms of a contractual arrangement between central and local government".[2]

Council told it faces 'big stick' in challenge on sale of houses

By Penny Chorlton

Sweeping powers had been given to the Environment Secretary under the 1980 Housing Act, Lord Dening said yesterday in the High Court. "It's a very, very, strong power," he said, adding: "It looks like a very big stick to me."

The Master of the Rolls had been told that Mr Michael Heseltine was legally entitled to move in and take over the functions and finances of Norwich City Council over its sale of council houses. But he could do this only if he had been certain that the councillors were dragging their feet to such an extent that tenants' rights under the Act to purchase their homes had been threatened.

This had not been the case, said Mr Nigel McLeod, QC, counsel for Norwich, which is appealing against a divisional court ruling. Last month, the divisional court rejected the council's claim that Mr Heseltine had acted unreasonably and illegally in taking over council house sales because of delays.

Mr McLeod said: "The council made no secret of its view that this Act is not wise legislation, but it has also said quite categorically that it intends to implement it and abide by the law."

He told Lord Denning and Lords Justice May and Kerr that the Housing Act had barely been in existence before the "bullying" by the Secretary of State began.

TheLabour-controlled council had started issuing notices under the Act to tenants who were entitled to buy, but delays had been inevitable when it came to accurate valuations, he said.

Lord Denning said he had never before seen a piece of legislation which gave such power to a minister.

"It's the first time it's been done under this Act, and I'm not aware of any comparable powers," said Mr McLeod.

The takeover had not hap-

pened, he said, but a team of Whitehall officials was waiting tomove in. "The council are carrying on and he's waiting for the case to be decided," he said.

Even before the Act became law the council had agreed that there were other urgent priorities in the housing area. A large number of people were on the waiting list and others needed transfers. With reduced staff because of economies imposed by Whitehall, it was inevitable that things would move slowly, said Mr McLeod.

In addition, the 748 tenants who had indicated that they wanted to buy meant that property worth about £20 million was at stake. It had been crucial to make the right valuations.

A further complication involved a row of 30 terrace houses on the outskirts of the city centre. The council had not wanted to sell these because the group as a whole was of historic and architectural interest. Time had been spent in trying to get ministerial permission to keep them under the 1933 Norwich Corporation Act.

Last September, the council had told 60 tenants that they could buy their homes for a specified price determined by the district valuer.

After several meetings and lengthy correspondence Mr Heseltine had told the council that he proposed, under the Act, to take over its powers. He told it that a two-year deadline for the completion of valuations was unacceptable.

"The letter hinted at surcharging councillors if they delayed," said Mr McLeod.

"Virtually, he's dictating to the council how they are carrying out their duties," commented Lord Denning. To let the houses go at too low a price would be a very serious matter, he said, adding that stock worth £20 million was a great deal to dispose of within a month or two.

The case continues on Monday.

102

On 21 December, Lord Denning, Master of the Rolls, sitting with Lord Justice Shaw and Lord Justice Ackner in the Appeal Court granted an application by Norwich, supported by the Secretary of State for the Environment to hear the appeal as soon as possible. The Minister had indicated that he would not intervene immediately provided the council acted "with due diligence" in seeking an urgent hearing of the appeal.

The appeal

The case came before Lord Denning (Master of the Rolls), Lord Justice Kerr and Lord Justice May in the Court of Appeal on Wednesday, 20 January. It went on until the following Wednesday. The length of the hearing seemed to confirm the view that there were important issues at stake and that the matter was not quite as clear cut as the judgement in the Divisional Court might have suggested. As the hearing progressed Norwich became more confident. Nigel Macleod had made a lot of progress particularly on the question of the appellate role of the District Valuer. There was a feeling that Denning was sympathetic to the Norwich case - siding with the underdog against the draconian powers of the Secretary of State. By late afternoon of Tuesday 26 Norwich felt they were on a winner and were looking forward to Nigel Macleod winding up the case the following morning. They noticed worried faces in the DOE camp.

But the next morning Simon Brown, acting for the Secretary of State, managed to retrieve an enormous amount of ground. A lot of extra work had apparently been done the previous evening. In particular, Brown succeeded in significantly undermining the objection to the use of the District Valuer by drawing parallels with his appellate role in the determination of rates. By the end of the day Norwich remained hopeful but rather less confident. Judgement was reserved and Norwich had to wait until 9 February for the verdict. During the course of the hearing the Lords judgement on the GLC "Fares Fair" policy had been delivered. Local government, constitutional issues and the role of the judiciary in political controversies were very much in the news.

Lord Denning delivered the leading judgement. In doing so he began by acknowledging the inherently political nature of the disagreement. But party politics and political views, he said, "are put aside in this court". The development of council housing and its future role had in recent years become the subject of much controversy. He reflected on the Clay Cross case, commenting with arguable political neutrality that "the local council used to let their council houses at very low rents" (our emphasis). Parliament, he said, "passed the Housing Finance Act 1972 requiring them to increase the rents up to sums which were fair". Briefly, describing the outcome of that conflict he went on to outline the nature of the Right to Buy legislation and the circumstances which led up to the present court proceedings. In Norwich there "seemed to be endless delays":

> "The tenants became very upset. They complained to the Secretary of State about the slowness. The Secretary of State tried to get the city council to hurry things up, but not with any great success. At length he took very drastic action. He took all the sales out of the hands of the council and into his own hands. The council dispute his right to do this. They have come to the court asking that the order of the Secretary of State be quashed".

Having summarised the views of the Secretary of State, Norwich officers and members and the tone of tenants' complaints, Denning then turned to the law. He had referred earlier to Section 23 as a most "unusual" power. He now described it as "a most coercive power". Its generic term was "a default power".* Denning commented that unlike other statutes where there were similar powers there were no provisions for the protection of the local authority. Section 95(3) of the Housing Finance Act 1972, for example, gave an opportunity for the local authority to be heard before a default order was made. This power, he said,

> "enables the central government to interfere with a high hand over local authorities". He went on, "Local self-government is such an important part of our constitution that to my mind the courts should be vigilant to see that this power of the central government is not exceeded or misused. Wherever the

---

* There appears to be ground for disagreement on this. M. Loughlin (1983) in Local Government, The Law and the Constitution, Local Government Legal Society Trust, suggests that it is "somewhat inaccurate" to characterise Section 23 power as a default power since "it is exercisable even if the local authority are not in default in carrying out their duties (p62).

> wording of the statute permits, the courts should read
> into it a provision that the 'default power' should not be
> exercised except in accordance with the rules of
> natural justice...... Simple fairness requires that this
> (Section 23 intervention) should not be done unless they
> are told what is alleged against them and they have had
> an opportunity of answering it".

Moreover, Denning added, the decision itself is open to judicial review if the Minister in using such powers "does not act in good faith, or if he acts on extraneous considerations which ought not to influence him, or if he misdirects himself in fact or in law...." The reasonable [our emphasis] behaviour of a local authority was also an issue in similar cases. If a Minister is interfering with a decision of a local authority "to which they came quite reasonably and sensibly" the court could intervene to prevent such interference. If however a local authority is behaving unreasonably, then such intervention may be justified. From this perspective it seemed that a judgement of whether or not Norwich had behaved reasonably was indeed relevant to the case (contrary to the views expressed in the Divisional Court). In Denning's view, the default power conferred on the Secretary of State under Section 23 should only be exercised after informing Norwich of the complaints, giving them a fair hearing but

> "even then he should not make the default order unless
> their default was unreasonable or, shall I say,
> inexcusable. Any other view would give the central
> government too much power over the elected
> representatives of the people".

The use of these powers must be subject to control by the courts.

Denning then went on to discuss the legitimate role of the District Valuer. Many councils had used the DV for initial valuations and this had speeded up the processing of applications. "But the Norwich City Council said this was not legitimate". Denning then rehearsed the objections Norwich had made regarding the appellate role of the DV. "That point" said Denning "impressed me much for some time. It seemed contrary to the accepted principle that justice must not only be done but should manifestly and undoubtedly be seen to be done". But Simon Brown, acting for the Secretary of State had done a good job in undermining this objection by drawing parallels with the District Valuer's appellate role in the determination of rates. If there is an appeal regarding valuations for rating then a different member of the DV's staff, the officer or his deputy, deals with the appeal. Denning observed that that system "works perfectly well in rating cases". Moreover it seemed in Denning's eyes to work perfectly well in relation to council house sales. Not only did it result in a great number of reduced valuations (a measure it seems of efficiency) but "no tenant (had) ever taken objection to the system". Indeed, emphasised Denning, of all the tenants and local authorities in the country only Norwich City Council had objected:

> "So justice is in fact done by reason of the final valuation being done by a senior officer quite distinct from the one who made the initial valuation. It is seen to be done by reason of the fact that no tenant has ever complained of it".

How did these general principles apply to the present case? Denning identified the three parties concerned:

> "First, the tenants of council houses who have the right to buy their houses from the council.

> Second, the local council who are under a duty to carry through the sale to the tenants effectively and expeditiously.

> Third, the Minister who is concerned to see that the council do their duty in that regard - and has power to issue a 'default order' if they do not do so".

Seen in this way it was not quite clear who was David and who was Goliath. Norwich were pleading their case in terms of the autonomy of democratically elected little government against centralist, insensitive big government. But for Denning the priorities were unambiguous. The concern of the court was to protect the individual from the abuse of institutional power. "The individual here is the tenant". According to Denning, tenants in Norwich wishing to exercise their Right to Buy had met with "intolerable" delay. Norwich had been misguided and ill advised. They should have used the District Valuer and streamlined their valuation procedures in other ways. "They acted - or failed to act - in complete good faith". Too little concern was shown for the rights of tenants. "They should have given them higher priority". The test of reasonableness was indeed relevant. Norwich had been unreasonable. It mattered little it seems that much of the justification by Norwich for the low priority given to sales was the high priority given to the needs of the majority of tenants who did not apparently wish to buy or to ratepayers by securing the best value for the sale of assets. Could it not have been interpreted that Norwich were indeed acting reasonably to protect the general interests of their tenants and ratepayers?

It seems not. The interests of tenants were necessarily narrowly defined as those wishing to buy their council house. If they were experiencing unreasonable delays they did not have recourse to the courts in this instance. "Nothing could be done effectively by mandamus". The remedy was contained in the statute. It was a "very great power" but one that had been used "after careful consideration". Denning concluded:

> "We were told that, pending these proceedings, the Secretary of State had allowed the Norwich City Council to carry on with the selling of the houses, and had not taken them out of their hands. This holds out hope for a solution. Surely the City Council will agree now to use the District Valuers to make the initial valuations. Surely they will speed up the procedure so as to avoid any further complaints. If they do this, there may be no need for the Secretary of State to act upon his order. But that his order was good, I have no doubt. I would dismiss this appeal".

Lord Justice Kerr's judgement began by pointing to the "unfortunate but inescapable feature" of Section 23 which was that it envisaged "a direct confrontation between the central government and local authorities". Much of the basis of this confrontation derived from the "powerful incentives" on offer to tenants to buy as soon as possible against the broader based priorities of the landlord, the local authority. In Kerr's view, "the local authority may reasonably consider that its many other duties and functions deserve a higher priority in the use of its resources than expediting the sale of council properties, to that proportion of the tenants who wish to buy". But in many ways such issues were outside the purview of the court. It was not a question of political position; whether the local authority or central government was in the right; or a judgement in favour of tenants. The court's duty was "solely to construe the relevant provisions of the Act and to determine whether the Minister's exercise of his powers under Section 23 was lawful or not".

In Kerr's view there was some doubt as to whether Section 23 was "penal" in nature but it was certainly "draconian". Its application could have "substantial consequences for the authority's funds in the housing sector, and therefore also for the general body of ratepayers". The scope and nature of the power was such that it required "a strict construction". What was being said was that the exercise of such powers should be liable to close scrutiny by the courts. But in fact there was little scope for judicial review. As Kerr commented:

> "Section 23 has clearly been framed by Parliament in such a way as to maximise the power of the Secretary of State and to minimise any power of review by the court".

And he went on:

> "The governing words are 'where it appears to the Secretary of State....' These words make it clear that the determinative factor is the view of the Secretary of State; not the view of the local authority in question; nor any abstract standard of reasonableness to be determined by the court".

As Loughlin has observed, "Government lawyers obviously had learnt their lessons from previous cases reviewing the exercise of discretionary power by Ministers".[3] They had taken no chances with a piece of legislation which was almost certain to be challenged in court.

Kerr then reviewed case law which involved the exercise of similar default powers. In other legislation there had been more scope for judicial review and the extent to which the authority had acted reasonably had indeed been relevant. But in Section 23 of the Housing Act where it <u>appeared</u> (our emphasis) that tenants were having difficulty exercising their Right to Buy effectively and expeditiously the Secretary of State could intervene whether or not this was due to the unreasonable conduct of the authority. In that sense Kerr observed that it (Section 23) "may well be without precedent in legislation of this nature". Whereas Denning had considered it appropriate to judge the behaviour of Norwich as unreasonable Kerr considered it unnecessary to pursue the question. Rather he was "driven" to the conclusion that the question was an altogether different one. Could the Minister have reasonably concluded on 3 December 1981 that tenants in Norwich "in fact or might have" difficulty in exercising their Right to Buy effectively and expeditiously?

Kerr illustrated his point with reference to the letter written by Len Stevenson to Michael Heseltine on 11 November. This, Kerr remarked, showed "the profound difference of approach as between the council and the Minister". In that letter Stevenson had forcefully put the council's position:

"It simply will not do, in our judgement, to neglect the problems of the homeless, and other statutory housing obligations - and the work we are doing to create employment - and combat other problems - just to enable a relatively small number of people, who are already comfortably housed, to buy a property a few months earlier than they otherwise could, when they will lose nothing by waiting".

Whilst Kerr thought the words "lose nothing by waiting" were rather an overstatement, this point was of no consequence. "The point for present purposes is that in my view the council could not possibly be regarded as having acted unreasonably in approaching its obligations under the Act on that basis. But this is not the relevant question under Section 23". The question was whether the Secretary of State could reasonably have drawn the conclusion that he did. In Kerr's view there was no doubt that the Secretary of State could have reasonably concluded that tenants in Norwich were experiencing difficulty buying their dwellings. He pointed to the clear evidence that the council's policy in relation to the sales of council houses was not only unenthusiastic but could be described as "passive resistance". He gave as a prime example the warning given during counselling of prospective purchasers that the right to resell after five years might disappear with the return of a Labour government.

It was not unreasonable for Norwich to take this view but in doing so it ran the risk of invoking Section 23. Kerr also commented on the fact that the minority party in Norwich had interpreted the situation in much the same way as the Secretary of State. Given that a group of councillors "who were fully familiar with the local situation" had reached the conclusion that prospective buyers were experiencing unreasonable delays it was "**a priori** difficult to see why the Minister could not reasonably have reached the same conclusion".

Had the Secretary of State been unreasonable in taking into account matters which had not been fully discussed with Norwich councillors and members? This referred to the objections about overpricing and onerous covenants. Kerr felt there was no obligation on the part of the Minister or the Department to become involved in argument on every point of detail. "Indeed, one of the draconian aspects of Section 23 is that it does not require any prior process of consultation or warning before the notice which brings it into effect".

And he had little sympathy with the objection put forward by Macleod that comparisons of performance between Norwich and other authorities were unreasonable - that circumstances varied so substantially that such measures were untenable. These comparisons had only extended "to other authorities to which similar warnings had also already been given". Comparative performance was a legitimate measure as "one of the ingredients" justifying intervention. And he added, "He [the Secretary of State] would certainly have been criticised if he had not done so".

But, like Denning, it was the legal issues around the use of the District Valuer which had been the most difficult. They had caused Kerr "the greatest anxiety". The crucial question in this area was whether it was unlawful to resort to the District Valuer. If so and if the Minister had in fact based his decision to intervene on the council's refusal to make use of the DV then "it cannot be doubted that his decision would have to be set aside". Kerr carefully stressed the basis for intervention. Once again it emerged that Norwich had been fighting the wrong battle. The Secretary of State's affidavit had explicitly stated that the decision to intervene "was in no way based on their reluctance to use the services of the District Valuer for Section 10 purposes".

This was perhaps as well. While Kerr had no doubt as to the legality of using the DV for such purposes he expressed an opinion that:

> "Although....resort to the District Valuer's officer at the Section 10 stage was not, and would in this case not have been, unlawful, I think that I might well have been driven to the conclusion that the Minister's decision should nevertheless be set aside if he had insisted on the council using the District Valuer at the Section 10 stage and had then based his decision to intervene under Section 23 on the ground that the council refused to do so. If this had happened, then - in view of the understandable doubt about the legal position - I might well have concluded that the basis of the Minister's

decision was sufficiently unreasonable to entitle the
court to set it aside".

But this had not been the case. Indeed at the meeting between
Norwich and Stanley and Heseltine on 5 November it had been
made clear that it was for Norwich to decide whether or not to use
the DV to speed up progress. Ministers and the DOE officers had
clearly been well advised on the appropriate strategy to avoid any
legal pitfalls. Kerr dismissed the appeal.

Lord Justice May delivered the final judgement and restricted his
comments to a few of the more important points which had arisen
during the proceedings. In particular he was less convinced of the
width of the powers given under Section 23. He had little doubt
that Section 23 was not 'penal' in nature and felt that the financial
consequences of intervention had been exaggerated by Nigel
Macleod. He also took up the issue of whether the reasonable or
unreasonable behaviour of Norwich was of relevance to the
invoking of Section 23. In May's view:

> "in construing Section 23 there is no need to insert any
> word that is not already there, that I cannot agree that
> the Secretary of State is only empowered by one
> section to issue a notice under it in circumstances
> where it can be said that the relevant local authority
> has acted unreasonably".

Here he parted company somewhat from Lord Denning who had
drawn on Lord Brandon's judgment in the case of **Bromley LBC v
The Greater London Council (1982)** to suggest that one of the
justifications for intervention was the unreasonable behaviour of
Norwich City Council. In May's view Brandon was referring to a
different question from the one being considered in the Norwich
case:

> "....Lord Brandon took the view that the courts could
> interfere where it could be shown that a local authority
> was acting in a way in which no reasonable local
> authority would act, so also would the courts interfere
> in a case such as the present if the Secretary of State
> took a decision to intervene under Section 23 in
> circumstances in which no reasonable Secretary of
> State would do so. It in no way follows from this
> proposition, nor indeed from the wording and scope of
> Section 23 of the 1980 Act, that a Secretary of State is
> only entitled to intervene when the relevant local

authority, in its turn, is acting unreasonably, that is to say is acting in a way in which no other reasonable local authority would act".

May's final comments related to the use of the District Valuer. Whilst understanding the suggested reasons for the council's objection to the use of the DV he also felt that Norwich "was not averse from taking the stance which it did to increase the delay to which this subjected its tenants". But he rejected the objections put forward by Nigel Macleod for much subtler reasons. In May's interpretation of Sections 10 and 11 of the Housing Act there could be no conflict between the appellate functions under Section 11 and determinations under Section 10 since Section 10 notices were only offers:

> "In the procedure prescribed by the Act, until the stage of Section 11 is reached, there has not been a 'determination' by the local authority which can be appealed from. The notice under Section 10 to be given by the local authority to its tenant is in my opinion merely an offer and in giving assistance to that local authority about the value of the material property under Section 6 of the Act, it is I think quite clear that the District Valuer would be acting in no respect in any partisan way, for or against the local authority".

The appeal was dismissed with costs.

Norwich had now lost all five judgements (two in the Divisional Court and three in the Court of Appeal). The objections to the use of the District Valuer had it seems been comprehensively undermined and rejected. While judgements on this had varied somewhat the parallels drawn with the procedures for appeal under the General Rating Law had proved to be the most persuasive weapon against the Norwich case. Without the late intervention by Simon Brown, Norwich might have won the argument on that particular issue.

But more significantly it is evident that the scope for legal resistance to intervention under Section 23 was severely restricted. Norwich had assumed that proof of their reasonable behaviour under the circumstances would be highly relevant to the eventual outcome of the legal proceedings. At the meeting of 10 November Tony Glover had suggested that while there was no definition in the Act of 'effectively and expeditiously' the question to be asked would be something like "Is what the council is doing reasonable?" In fact some of the judgements concluded that it was. Unfortunately it proved to be an irrelevant question.

6
THE AFTERMATH

The judgement of the Court of Appeal as delivered on 9 February 1982 was by no means the end of the Norwich council house sales saga. But nor did the subsequent saga prove entirely predictable. Norwich could have appealed and could have refused to cooperate. The Secretary of State could have set up a parallel alternative administration perhaps using private firms. The experience of the period after the Appeal Court judgement is of interest for various reasons and illustrates the practical problem and impact of a central government 'take over' of local administration.

Further appeal?

Norwich City Council decided against making a further appeal to the House of Lords following the judgement in February. Norwich could have petitioned the House of Lords to seek a further appeal and discussion in the Court of Appeal had identified this as the quickest way of obtaining a hearing before the House of Lords.

The City Council decided not to petition the House of Lords. They did this for two reasons. Firstly, the balance of legal advice suggested that they would not win. Secondly the costs of such an appeal were very high. Following this decision two stances were possible. Norwich could have refused to cooperate and left the Secretary of State to get on with the job. Alternatively Norwich could say the law is the law, the courts have decided, and start from that position to sort out arrangements as amicably as possible. The second stance had a variety of advantages. It was consistent with the spirit of the appeal in which Norwich had always denied any obstructionist approach to the policy; it would make DOE appear unreasonable if they did not operate equally amicably and constructively; and it offered a greater prospect of safeguarding the financial and other interests of Norwich in this matter. The use of private agencies would have been expensive

**Department of the Environment
City Hall
NORWICH NR2 1NH**
Telephone: Norwich (0603) 612522

Norwich concedes defeat on house sales

By Ian Black

Norwich City Council has conceded defeat in its battle over council house sales with the Environment Secretary and has decided against petitioning the House of Lords over the ruling against it by the Court of Appeal.

On Tuesday, Lord Denning and his fellow judges unanimously rejected the council's challenge to Mr Michael Heseltine's takeover of the sale of council houses to tenants exercising the right to buy.

The Environment Secretary argued that Norwich failed to act quickly and effectively to satisfy tenants' purchase rights under the 1980 Housing Act. He sent in his own agents to do the job and warned the council that they could be surcharged for the costs.

Mr Heseltine's right to take such action was upheld by the High Court and then by the Court of Appeal. The council was ordered to pay the estimated £20,000 costs involved in the proceedings and refused leave to appeal to the Lords.

Mr Len Stevenson, the leader of the Labour-controlled council, said last night: "There didn't seem any point in pursuing the matter further. With the two High Court judges and the three Appeal Court judges, it is five-nil against us."

SALE OF HOUSES TERMS

Environment Secretary Mr. Michael Heseltine yesterday announced the terms on which he had consented to Norwich City Council continuing to process the sale of council houses.

The announcement followed the recent decision by the Court of Appeal upholding his right of intervention.

In a written reply to Mr. Paul Hawkins, MP for South-West Norfolk, Mrs. Heseltine said, "while maintaining my notice of intervention in force, I have consented to the continued processing of sales by the Norwich City Council to a timetable and on conditions which I have laid down as follows:

"1. The council should issue all their outstanding section 10 notices by March 31st, 1982, including the so-called 'difficult' cases, and should complete sales of all cases by such dates as I consider the earliest practicable in the circumstances, generally June 30th, 1982 where the right to buy has now been admitted.

REPORTS

2. All questions involving the exercise of discretion, such as service charges, covenants in leases and so on, are to be referred to me.

3. Weekly progress reports are to be submitted to me against a programme to be worked out after consultation between officials of the department and the council.

4. The department is to be given access to case papers and processes as required by the department to ensure that all matters are proceeding satisfactorily. Accommodation is to be provided in the City Hall for one of my staff for this purpose.

5. The city council will be responsible for the cost incurred by me for the intervention arrangements from December 7th, 1981, until the notice of intervention is withdrawn."

Mr. Heseltine said the city council had accepted these arrangements.

115

and Norwich would have lost control over financial aspects and, more specifically, lost the interest on payments for house purchase. The City Council had already discussed this aspect.[1] In this sense a decision to accept the judgement and cooperate was not capitulation but a response consistent with a stubborn insistence on representing local interests.   The financial consideration in this is of great importance.   As was outlined in Chapter 2, Section 23 of the Housing Act 1980 empowers the Secretary of State, following intervention, to receive any sums due to the landlord (as mortgagee). The Secretary of State is not bound to account to the landlord for any interest accruing and is entitled to charge the landlord for any costs. In this way Norwich found itself in February 1982 facing potentially large financial penalties. The costs of losing the legal action would be enormously increased by such penalties.

These considerations influenced Norwich's decision to cooperate fully with the Secretary of State.   Immediately following the appeal decision, the council decided not to appeal further and wrote offering to cooperate fully.   The view within the City Council was that the DOE had not expected this cooperation. Indeed the DOE had already rented premises and promised to use private sector agencies to process sales.   Replying to a parliamentary question on 28 January Mr Stanley had stated that the cost of setting up a government office in Norwich had, up to then, been £2,523.80.   This covered office costs for two months from 7 December, secretarial, and cleaning services and telephone rental but excluded the cost of telephone calls and electricity charges.[2]   Norwich's offer of cooperation rendered such arrangements (and the costs they implied for Norwich) unnecessary.   Indeed, for the DOE to have persisted with them would have appeared unreasonable. Consequently the DOE set up its office within the council buildings.

The letterhead read:

Department of the Environment
City Hall
Norwich NR2 1NH

The office consisted only of the Secretary of State's representative and his secretary - the cooperation of Norwich was such that a larger staff (and its costs) was not required. And the control over the administration of sales was retained within the local authority. In order to meet the representative's demands, Norwich took on additional staff, staff worked overtime and the city made use of the District Valuer for initial valuations. The officer responsible had calculated that if the work had been sent out it would have cost over £23,000 in fees. Through the cooperation of the council's conveyancers who worked substantial overtime, the same task was done for about £3,000. Because the local authority processed sales the proceeds from such sales went directly to Norwich. While the DOE charged Norwich for its costs it did not receive any sums from sales or any interest associated with these. Sales continued to go through the Housing Committee and Mortgages (Joint) Sub-Committee as before.

In a parliamentary reply on 23 February Mr Heseltine stated:

"Whilst maintaining my notice of intervention in force, I have consented to the continued processing of sales by the Norwich city council to a timetable and on conditions which I have laid down as follows:

The council should issue all its outstanding section 10 notices by 31 March, 1982, including so-called 'difficult' cases, and should complete sales in all cases by such dates as I consider the earliest practicable in the circumstances, generally by 30 June, 1982 where the right-to-buy has now been admitted.

All questions involving the exercise of discretion, such as service charges, convenants in leases and so on, are to be referred to me.

Weekly progress reports are to be submitted to me against a programme to be worked out after consultation between officials of the Department and the council.

The Department is to be given access to case papers and processes as required by the Department to ensure that all matters are proceeding satisfactorily. Accommodation is to be provided in the city hall for one of my staff for this purpose.

The city council will be responsible for the cost incurred by me under the intervention arrangements from 7 December 1981 until the notice of intervention is withdrawn."

Mr Heseltine stated that the city council had accepted these arrangements.[3]

This decision followed a letter from the Chief Executive to Mr Heseltine offering to process Right to Buy applications in a manner and at a rate which would be entirely acceptable to the Secretary of State.[4] The General Purposes Committee meeting on 16 February had supported this approach even though it could include using the District Valuer, taking on temporary staff, overtime working or contracting work out. The council Leader Len Stevenson was reported as saying:

> "I hope that when the Minister takes his decision on the letter we have sent him he will bear in mind that our conduct throughout the affair, despite strong disagreements, has been honourably conducted and will continue to be so".[5]

Following Mr Heseltine's decision Mr Stevenson was reported in the press:

> "If the Minister is going to let us do the work then he must be reasonably sure that we are keeping our word".

The press report continued:

> "A DOE spokesman said the office set up in the city to deal with house sales would not be used if the council agreed to the time limit, but buyers would be able to go there for advice".[6]

Press reports of a meeting to clarify the final details stated:

> "The council agreed to Mr Michael Heseltine's demands to complete applications to buy from tenants by the end of March, and to complete sales by the end of June.
>
> About 12 extra staff are to be taken on to do the work, which should earn the council in the region of £5 million.
>
> Around 50 houses have already been sold, netting £500,000, and 800 or so more sales should be completed within the next few months.
>
> Housing committee chairman Mr David Fullman said he hoped the council would be able to deal with about 120 applications a week.

"We should break the back of them by the middle of March. We hope to have done about 380 by 24 March" said Mr Fullman.

He complimented Mr Edye on the 'amicable' talks between the council and DOE. "I feel that if we had had the attitude all the way through that we have had today from Mr Edye things would never have gone as far as they did".

Labour leader Mr Stevenson said he was glad the city council had resisted the government. "At least we tried and I think it was an honourable defeat".

He said the people on council waiting lists would suffer, especially as selling homes would deplete the housing stock.

Money from selling council houses would not be used to build new ones, he said".[7]

In this stage of the process the DOE through its Norwich office intervened over certain detailed aspects of sales. As well as insisting on a timetable for completion of valuations and conveyances the DOE wanted to make changes to key documents (conveyance, lease, mortgage). Considerable time was spent 'negotiating' over the treatment of district heating, service arrangements, horticultural maintenance, common areas and decorative repair.

In this situation the officers of Norwich city council saw their role as to be non-alarmist and to accept and parry DOE proposals in a logical way - forcing DOE to find suitable arguments for persisting. The spirit of cooperation made Norwich stronger in this respect. In their view DOE officials were unfamiliar and inexperienced in practical policy administration, learned from their experience in Norwich and consulted Norwich over matters arising elsewhere. And this process further led such officials to accept the integrity of Norwich officers. These officers felt there was a build up of trust although there were also irritating and time wasting negotiations on matters of detail.

Norwich officers had views on other aspects of the administration of sales following the implementation of intervention. The inexperience of civil servants, the constant reference of matters of detail to Ministers, an occasional spiteful or smug attitude by some civil servants, and a tendency to regard Norwich as left of centre politically were perceived as obstacles by Norwich officers in carrying out their tasks. On the other hand the personality and reasonableness of the Secretary of State's representative enabled an effective working relationship. On balance, however, the 'quibbles' and detailed legal aspects insisted on by DOE (and not operated in other local authority areas) delayed progress and made the work associated with sales more difficult. In this view the volume of sales achieved between March 1982 and March 1983 was achieved despite the DOE.

Looked at in this way it does seem that for the DOE the action in Norwich probably had its greatest impact (and this was no doubt the intention) in demonstrating political will, and encouraging others - rather than in achieving results for Norwich tenants. For the DOE the aim of the exercise was achieved in February 1982. There were no plaudits or honours to be earned from the subsequent administrative task. One Norwich view of DOE's position was that:

> "when they won in the Court of Appeal they'd have liked to have said, 'Oh, we've won, end of story, we don't want anything'. But they couldn't. They had this great, horrible mess that they had to deal with called the aftermath of the litigation and they had no stomach for that because there were no flags or rosettes being awarded on that one. From there on out they were losing. They'd had their day in February and from there on out it was a question of making smartie points if they could and they didn't because it was difficult for them".[8]

Had DOE been left to administer the system without full cooperation from Norwich, the lack of experience of DOE and the private sector could have seriously exposed the intervention. The localist concern of Norwich and lack of political recalcitrance and distinctive political militancy prevented this from being the case. But the conclusion to be drawn is about both the strength and weakness of the mechanism being adopted for central government. Its strength is demonstrated in the successful challenge to local views of priorities. Its weakness is at the same time evident in the exercise in brinkmanship and the risk that the competence of central government would be exposed by being left to carry out local administration. In such a case the image of the Secretary of State's representative, rather than that of being a reasonable and effective check on an independent local administration, could have come closer to that of a gauleiter or commissar. At this point it is worth clarifying the status of the Secretary of State's representative. Under the Housing Finance Act 1972 the Minister had had the power formally to appoint a Commissioner - vesting specific powers in that person. Under the Housing Act 1980 the Secretary of State is the person with the power to act. There is no person formally vested with statutory powers to do things in their own right rather than acting under the authority of the Secretary of State. For this reason it can be argued that in strictly formal terms it was not a commissioner who was appointed but a representative of the Secretary of State. This distinction is not one which is generally recognised and the Secretary of State's representative tends to be referred to as a commissioner.

Progress with sales

By 12 February 1982 Norwich had received 1,041 claims under the Right to Buy. It had completed only 111 sales - representing some 11% of claims. Tables 3 to 5 provide details of the progress of sales in the twelve months following intervention. The initial impact of the intervention is apparent in relation to the issue of Section 10 notices (notice of valuation and purchase price). The number of notices issued had doubled by June 1982 reflecting overtime and staffing arrangements. By June 84% of claimants had received a Section 10 notice. As there had been 79 withdrawn claims this represented 90% of 'active' claims. Perhaps more significantly the claims still awaiting Section 10 notices were all 'recent' claims. In February 454 of 915 active claims had had Section 10 notices issued. By 21 April 13 of these cases had been withdrawn and only four of the active claims from February had not yet been the subject of a Section 10 notice. By 2 June all the backlog of claims had been removed and the rate of processing was keeping pace with new applications. This rate of progress can be contrasted with the rate Norwich had said was feasible without incurring additional staff costs. A rate of 60 per month from February 1982 would have implied no increase at all in the rate of processing Section 10 notices compared with the period since October. At this rate the backlog of claims in February would not have been cleared by October 1982 (see Table 4). But by then over 600 other cases would have accumulated - representing a ten month queue. Indeed, new cases arose at more than 60 a month in the period after February 1982. In this sense Norwich had not received the bulk of RTB claims by February 1983 and the projected rate of progress would have dealt with only some 61% of

Table 3:
Norwich's progress after intervention:
Claims and acceptances

	Claims received	RTB 2s issued	Acceptances issued
Up to 12.2.82	1041	1024	970
Up to 3.3.82	1112	1037	983
Up to 21.4.82	1322	1242	1176
Up to 2.6.82	1475	1371	1299
Up to 7.7.82	1545	1485	1408
Up to 1.9.82	1689	1618	1539
Up to 6.10.82	1809	1717	1637
Up to 3.11.82	1908	1803	1722
Up to 1.12.82	2008	1922	1839
Up to 5.1.83	2079	1977	1889
Up to 2.2.83	2191	2094	2002
At 31.12.83	2821	2660	

NB A small number of those accepting offers subsequently withdrew.
By 2.2.83 there were 30 such cases and 4 deferred completions.

122

Table 4:
Norwich's progress after intervention:
Section 10 notices

	Notices required[1]	Notices issued	Notices issued as a percentage of those required	Proposed rate of issue by Norwich[2]
12.1.82	915	454	50	454
3.3.82	918	511	56	514
21.4.82	1098	898	82	604
2.6.82	1220	1096	90	679
7.7.82	1327	1196	90	754
1.9.82	1457	1385	95	859
6.10.82	1555	1447	93	934
3.11.82	1637	1553	95	994
1.12.82	1755	1639	93	1054
5.1.83	1805	1725	96	1114
2.2.83	1918	1803	94	1174

[1] RTB acceptances less withdrawals before Section 10 stage.

[2] This is an estimate based on the offer made by Norwich to DOE of 60 Section 10 notices issued each month.

Table 5:
Norwich's progress after intervention:
Sales completed

	Number of completions	Completions as percentage of acceptances	Completions as percentage of cases where offer terms acceptable
Up to 12.2.82	101	10	53
Up to 3.3.82	111	11	50
Up to 21.4.82	178	15	48
Up to 2.6.82	249	19	53
Up to 7.7.82	355	25	53
Up to 1.9.82	544	35	65
Up to 6.10.82	635	39	65
Up to 3.11.82	727	42	70
Up to 1.12.82	829	45	73
Up to 5.1.83	906	48	74
Up to 2.2.83	975	49	74
At 31.12.83	1639		

active cases by February 1983 - compared with the 94% actually achieved following the intervention.

From their stated views about priorities in administration it is unlikely that Norwich would have introduced special procedures once they realised that the 'hump of work' was a long one. It is apparent that the DOE intervention and Norwich's cooperation following the failure of the legal challenge did greatly accelerate the rate of processing sales. Such evidence does not, of course, add anything to the argument about priorities in expenditure and in carrying out the duties laid upon the City Council.

In this context it is not relevant to carry out an elaborate exercise to assess how Norwich's performance following the intervention compared with that of other authorities. It is relevant to note that at the end of 1982 comparative sales statistics show that the demand for purchase was low in Norwich. When claims under the Right to Buy are expressed as a percentage of the council stock there were only 31 authorities with a rate below the 7.4% for Norwich. And 14 of these authorities were London Boroughs. When completions are expressed as a percentage of the council stock even fewer authorities had a lower rate than Norwich's 3.6%. At the end of 1983 the picture remained similar. Some local authorities had sold 20% of their stock; the average rate of sales in England was 10% and in the Eastern region 12%. Norwich had sold 6%. Relatively low rates of completed sales could perhaps initially be attributed to some extent to political resistance. But once new procedures following the legal dispute had been established it became clear that low demand was also a very important factor.

Two other aspects merit brief reference. Firstly, Norwich in this period was not only affected by the Right to Buy. As with other local authorities reductions in resources available for housing investment declined rapidly. In 1980 over 600 new council dwellings were built by Norwich. In 1982 only 28 were completed. Other public sector completions had also declined and private sector completions had not increased. In 1980, 178 private sector completions were recorded; and in 1982, 190. Council house sales were the major element contributing to the growth of owner occupation and were also contributing to an actual decline in the council stock. Secondly, the pattern of sales was not uniform throughout the housing stock. The bulk of sales were of three bedroom houses and - partly reflecting this - the level of sales completed varied between estates. By January 1983 this ranged from nil in Vauxhall Street to 9.0% in Heartsease. By September

1984 three estates had still had fewer than 1% of dwellings sold. On Heartsease sales had risen to 19%. The implementation of policy was changing the size and structure of the council stock of which local councillors were - in almost everyone's view - justifiably proud.[9] In this sense the objections and fear of the way in which council house sales would erode the council stock have proved correct.

Withdrawal?

In spite of the progress made over council house sales the notice of intervention served in December 1981 was not withdrawn until May 1985. As early as July 1982 Norwich had written to state that all deadlines had been met and all points raised by DOE had been dealt with. In the light of that, it was argued, the intervention should be withdrawn. The refusal to withdraw again raises questions over the nature of the legislation and the intentions of central government. Applications to purchase had not ceased to come forward and a backlog of uncompleted cases remained. In addition one Norwich view was that the continuation of the intervention enabled DOE to educate itself over problems of local administration. The detailed experience of problems over conveyances, service charges and other aspects enabled DOE to press other authorities and to provide detailed advice based on their experience of Norwich. DOE officials consulted Norwich over problems arising in other authorities.

In December 1982 Norwich asked again for the intervention to be withdrawn. It appears that on this occasion the request was considered by Ministers and referred to Downing Street. One Norwich view was that civil service advice to Ministers reflected inexperience, weakness and lack of expertise. Ministers saw the issue as party political and continued to resent the challenge to government. But it must also be said that the decision to use the law as it was entitled to was not an unimportant one and that having set up a Norwich office a decision to withdraw could appear irresponsible if any doubts remained and if any tenants complained subsequently. In addition it must be remembered that this action was not determined solely by what was happening in Norwich. As has previously been noted in December 1983 the government was scrutinising the performance of about 200 local authorities in respect of the implementation of the Right to Buy. And the government in 1983 had introduced a new Housing Bill - the Housing and Building Control Bill - which was designed to extend and speed up council house sales.

Legislation for future conflict?

The Housing and Building Control Act 1984 was not introduced because of the Norwich intervention. Nevertheless there are aspects of the new legislation which represent a response to the kind of circumstances which led to the conflict and litigation involving Norwich. Part I of the Act comprises 38 of the 66 Sections of the Act. And of the 12 Schedules seven are concerned with Part I. Part I is concerned with the disposal of public sector dwelling-houses and the rights of secure tenants. In relation to disposals significant changes extend the Right to Buy to secure tenants of only two years standing (rather than three), extend discount arrangements for secure tenants of over 20 years' tenancy, extend the Right to Buy to certain properties where the landlord (the local authority) does not own the freehold or where the property is not held under Part V and define circumstances where the Right does not arise more strictly. These latter aspects can be seen as steps to close loopholes in the original legislation.

But for the purposes of this study four other changes to the law are more important. Firstly, Section 9 of the new Act provides a power for the Secretary of State to give directions on covenants and conditions included in grants or conveyances. Such a direction could apply to conveyances or grants which had already been executed. The power represents a mechanism for intervening over these issues - in the way which had been done in Norwich - without the clumsy procedure of introducing a commissioner.

Section 10 empowers the Secretary of State - where it appears necessary or expedient to consider using his powers of intervention - to serve a notice requiring the landlord to produce documents or supply information.

Section 11 empowers the Secretary of State to give assistance to persons claiming, exercising (or successors to those exercising) the Right to Buy, where this raises 'a question of principle', where complexity or other matters make it unreasonable to expect the applicant to cope without any assistance, or by reason of 'any other special consideration'. This applies to any aspect of the Right to Buy except for proceedings to determine valuation. The assistance the Secretary of State could provide includes giving advice, arranging for legal advice or assistance (including legal representation) and any other form of assistance which the Minister considers appropriate. The costs of providing such assistance would be met from costs in a legal judgement or by Parliament.

Finally, the Housing and Building Control Act reduces local discretions over the Right to Buy. Under the 1980 legislation landlords were able, when all relevant matters had been sorted out, to serve a notice requiring the tenant to complete the purchase within 28 days. The new legislation of 1984 extended this period to 56 days and removed the exclusion of a tenant who failed to complete, from serving a new notice claiming the Right to Buy. Prior to this an exclusion for the following 12 months could be applied. At the same time the legislation of 1984 required the landlord to meet a more stringent timetable in acknowledging the Right to Buy. Landlords are required to serve tenants with notice of the terms of the sale within eight weeks rather than 'as soon as is practicable'.

These sections of the Housing and Building Control Act 1984 provide central government with a more varied armoury of mechanisms for intervention than existed in the Norwich case. In the event of future conflicts the long drawn out, public and heavy handed procedure culminating in the introduction of a 'commissioner', could be avoided. Instead the Secretary of State could carry out legal processes on behalf of individuals - and be seen to be acting on behalf of the powerless individual rather than basking in the arrogant exercise of power on behalf of a centralised bureaucracy. The consequence seems likely to be an even greater shift of real power to the centre.

New legislation and continuing scrutiny of progress with the Right to Buy provides a continuing potential for central-local government conflict in this area. Nevertheless the Norwich saga strictly terminated on 7 May 1985. After a period of three and a half years the Secretary of State withdrew the notice of 3 December 1981. The notice of withdrawal is reproduced on page 129. The emphasis placed on being satisfied that tenants are and will continue to be able to exercise the Right to Buy effectively and expeditiously is fully consistent with the emphasis in earlier phases of the conflict.

In the aftermath of the service of notice of intervention Norwich had held on to administration and cooperated in the best interests of tenants and ratepayers. Although defeat in the courts was unfortunate and the notice had remained in operation longer than had been hoped Norwich can reasonably be regarded to have coped satisfactorily with the circumstances. For central government the outcome was more favourable. Success in the courts had strengthened their hand in relations with other authorities, closeness to detailed day to day administration had informed them

HOUSING ACT 1980: SECTION 23(6)
NOTICE OF WITHDRAWAL OF NOTICE OF INTERVENTION
BY THE SECRETARY OF STATE FOR THE ENVIRONMENT

To: The Council of the City of Norwich (hereinafter called
"the Council"), City Hall, Norwich NR2 1NH

WHEREAS by a Notice dated the 3rd December 1981 the Secretary
of State for the Environment (hereinafter called "the
Secretary of State") notified the Council of his intention
to use his powers under section 23 of the Housing Act 1980
(hereinafter called "the 1980 Act") to enable tenants of
the Council to exercise the right to buy and the right
to a mortgage and made the provision therein contained:

AND WHEREAS by virtue of a Consent of the Secretary of
State dated the 7th December 1981 (as modified) the Council
have processed applications made to them by persons claiming
to exercise the right to buy or the right to a mortgage:

AND WHEREAS the Secretary of State being satisfied from
reports given to him by the Council that their tenants
are able to exercise the right to buy effectively and
expeditiously and from assurances given by the Council
that their tenants will in future be able to do so has
agreed to withdraw the said Notice:

NOW THEREFORE the Secretary of State in pursuance of the
powers conferred on him by section 23(6) of the 1980 Act
and of all other powers enabling him in that behalf,
HEREBY WITHDRAWS the said Notice dated the 3rd December 1981.

Signed by authority of   Minister for Housing and
the Secretary of State.   Construction,
                                Department of the Environment.
Date: 7 May, 1985

129

of problems and issues and again strengthened their position through increasing knowledge. At the same time the intervention had not been marked by any crisis or failure of administration. During the court proceedings although the Order was operative Norwich had been left to administer sales - avoiding any hiatus. And in the aftermath of legal judgement Norwich's attitude had prevented the full burden of administrative responsibility from falling on the Department. In the end it had proved valuable for the Department that there had been a challenge. Once judgement had been made the Department was better able to carry through its intentions in Norwich and in other areas. But a success for the Department in these terms should not obscure either the view that failure had been very close or that the conflict itself and its outcome was about constitutional and other issues rather than the Right to Buy alone.

7

THE END – OF LOCAL GOVERNMENT?

The Norwich council house sales saga informs a wide range of arguments. What is important at the outset, however, is to acknowledge that it was at the time a <u>cause celebre</u>. It was seen as a serious threat to the government, as a potential terminator of Ministerial careers and as one of a small number of testing acts in defence of local government and local control and in defiance of ever extending centralism. A detailed blow by blow account strips the celebrated case of some of its romance and much of its mythology. But this would probably happen if most of such cases were analysed in this way. The wisdom of hindsight makes it appear that Norwich was never likely to win. The very fact that the case was pursued by long standing, responsible councillors (not Johnny come latelys) with support from mature, hard-headed professional bureaucrats (hardly political adventurers) is the clearest denial of this. The action at the time was an important test and its outcome is of considerable importance. Nor was it ultimately a test of council house sales and housing policy. To see the saga in this perspective is to strip it of a real political context.

It became a constitutional issue and a test of the role of central government in the supervision and control of duties by legally independent local authorities. The resolution of the action represented a clear statement that the new legislation operating in this area of policy was framed in such a way as to significantly shift the traditional practice and balance of power in the exercise of power and duties by central and local government. In retrospect what leading actors within Norwich and advising Norwich, and what leading commentators outside failed to appreciate was the nature and extent of the shift facilitated by powers of intervention which were framed in an entirely new way.

131

Reasonable actions? Nationalising housing policy

One of the apparent ironies of this case is that both parties - central and local government - behaved reasonably. On the one hand, as indicated in the judgement of Kerr LJ, Norwich had not acted unreasonably in approaching its obligations under the Housing Act 1980. On the other hand the Secretary of State won the case. But this is a smokescreen. What it obscures is the nature of the legislation involved. The legislation in origin and draftsmanship represented a determined break with consensus and with the belief that local authorities were the best judges of local needs and policies. It represented an attack on social ownership and part of a wider policy to encourage owner occupation. In these terms it represented carrying forward onto the statute book the arguments, victories and defeats which had been experienced by Conservatives over a long period of time. And it represented a view that reasonable action by local authorities acting as landlords was no longer what was required. A laissez faire attitude towards landlord behaviour was not compatible with a view that local authorities should reduce their role as property owner and manager. The legislation rested upon a divergence of interest clearly reflected in Norwich - between maintaining and building on the housing role established in the city over 50 years and abandoning that tradition without benefiting from the realisation of the full asset values in council housing. The legislation is also significant in requiring actions which have cost implications at a time when controls over both capital and current expenditure were being increased.

In this sense what emerges is that Section 23 of the Housing Act 1980 represents an important departure from the tradition of legislation governing central-local relations. From the point of view of local government it is an unreasonable breach of that tradition. It does not represent a conventional default power. It is not default which was found in the Norwich case. Rather, it enables the Secretary of State to intervene even where default does not apply. And it provides the basis for a much wider central intervention in local policy than the conventional view has established.

It is worth elaborating on this briefly. Reference was made in Chapter 2 to the very large number of authorities 'listed' by DOE in connection with the Right to Buy. Contrast this with Griffith's account of the attitude of the central department responsible for housing - then the Ministry of Housing and Local Government - in the early 1960s. He described the philosophy of the Ministry regarding local government as laissez faire:

> "in that it leaves the local housing authorities to decide
> what is their local need, and how far (if at all) it is to
> be met".

Griffith went on to say that the Department had no machinery to discover whether programmes were realistic or reflected local needs:

> "no one....looks to see whether local housing authorities
> are fulfilling their statutory obligations. And in many
> cases, the local housing authorities do not know
> whether they are doing so because of the inadequacy of
> the means of assessing housing need".[1]

There were exceptions to this attitude and some of the Department's activities were regulatory (control of standards, layout and design) or promotional (advisory material, research and development). The Department was more inclined to encourage local autonomy and to restrict itself to exhortation and advice than other departments.

The Ministry of Housing and Local Government maintained a quasi-judicial role in conflicts between different local authorities and between local authorities and the public. This is perhaps most simply illustrated with reference to planning powers and procedures. Secondly, the Minister inherited a tradition which did not involve any inspection system. The origins of government activity in the nineteenth century development of public health provision were fraught with conflict over 'centralisation' and inspection in a manner which is distinct from that of the Department of Education and Science. Thirdly, housing legislation did not generally impose duties on local authorities comparable with those in other fields. The increasing concern of governments with the provision, condition and management of housing had not resulted in clear legislation laying down how far housing is a public service. Local authorities consequently could not easily be shown to be failing to meet responsibilities and the Ministry was not able to establish measures of standard which local authorities should meet.

The Department had not attempted to assess needs and control building or other activities. Accordingly, its functions had remained regulatory and its controls negative. Apart from some technical advice and the promotion of building in priority areas no exercise was undertaken comparable to that for school building or highway construction, to ensure that national resources were clearly seen to be expended where they were most needed. In view of this Griffith stated "that it would be most surprising if all local housing authorities were in fact fulfilling their statutory obligations or their public duties to clear unfit houses and to provide for housing needs of all kinds".[2]

Griffith stated that "unlike the Secretary of State for Education and Science, the Ministry of Housing and Local Government has no statutory duty to ensure that the community is better housed". The Department:

> "do not at present assume a national responsibility for housing building; do not assume the function of ensuring that local housing authorities are fulfilling their statutory obligations to provide housing accommodation to the extent that it is needed; and therefore do not seek to exercise over local authorities the same amount of control which is exercised by the departments responsible for school building or the country's roads".[3]

Throughout this period a major factor in central-local relations was Ministerial preoccupation with the annual rate of housing construction.

Evelyn Sharp, Permanent Secretary to the Ministry of Housing and Local Government from 1955 to 1966 has stated that successive Ministers were preoccupied with the annual rate of housing construction. In this environment it may be that the relevance of closer control or supervision was limited. Exhortation was the order of the day reflecting political priorities in housing. Intense political pressures and overwhelming current housing problems dominated and:

> "except in relation to the number of houses they may build, local authorities probably enjoy in relation to housing greater independence of Whitehall and more freedom to develop their own policies than in any other major service".[4]

But the situation has changed over the last fifteen years. In 1969 Evelyn Sharp stated that the Department had become increasingly interventionist because of perceived limitations of local authorities and 'political disagreement'. This interventionism had continued to increase with the Housing Finance Act, Housing Strategies and

Investment Programmes and disputes over council house sales being prime examples - again involving 'political disagreement'.

Since Griffith's view was developed circumstances have changed considerably. Housing cost yardsticks, design standards and project controls have all involved an increase in central control. The increasing role of regional offices following the formation of the Department of the Environment in 1970 has been associated with these controls and the development of controls over levels of spending under Section 105 of the Housing Act 1974 and subsequently Housing Strategies and Investment Programmes.

The increasing central government intervention in various aspects of housing including rents has partly been a product of political and ideological stances. It has also partly been related to economic crises and policies to cut and restrict public expenditure and borrowing. The development of expenditure controls, cash limits and the Housing Strategies and Investment Programmes system and the new subsidy system under the Housing Act 1980 are particularly important in this respect and seriously affect central-local government relationships.

Since 1964 governments have constantly attempted to develop a national policy for local housing services - to ensure that local policies conform collectively to national objectives. This attempt has been evident in the operation of ad hoc controls on expenditure. For example, in 1976 when new building was first subject to expenditure controls these were first relaxed for 'stress authorities'. Various specific programmes (including the Inner City Policy and Comprehensive Community Programmes) are examples of attempts to channel resources in particular directions. In 1978-79 £100m 'construction money' associated with Inner City policy was allocated (as permission to borrow) to the seven Inner City partnership authorities and 14 of the programme authorities to supplement expenditure. The most notable example in this area is the development of the Housing Strategies and Investment Programmes system in England and Wales and Housing Plans in Scotland.

From each of these developments it is clear that Griffith's laissez-faire view and Cullingworth's bargaining view are no longer sufficient.[5] The detail and complexity of controls have developed considerably and the growth in particular of financial controls significantly alters the relationship. Developments such as the Housing (Homeless Persons) Act 1977 and the obligations under the

Housing Defects Act 1984 have reduced the area of discretion. Most strikingly there has been an uneven development of control and scrutiny.

Bargaining has been seen as a central theme in central-local government relations. Policy action involves both parties; each requires the 'resources' of the other and consequently both are willing to negotiate. But it must be concluded that in the question of council house sales local authorities have no resources to bargain with. While there was a 'bargain' struck in the aftermath of legal action this was more a negotiation over the terms of surrender than a bargain struck between partners in an enterprise to deliver public service. Legislation and political determination at least in this area of policy has rendered the conventional accounts of the nature of central-local relations strangely out of touch with contemporary reality.

The central department still leaves local housing authorities to decide what is their local need and how far (if at all) it is to be met. In spite of the development of regional offices the Department still has no machinery or apparent desire to discover whether programmes submitted by local housing authorities reflect local needs or are appropriate. Moreover the housing programme since 1976 has not been open ended and has ceased to be even notionally based on local estimates of need, priorities and capacity to implement. HIP allocations and constraints on capital and revenue expenditure reflect central government's financial and public expenditure priorities rather than locally determined priorities.

Control and scrutiny has developed least in respect of measures of performance in meeting need. It has developed most in respect of controlling expenditure. The Right to Buy and the detailed scrutiny associated with it represents a striking departure from the philosophy described by Griffith. It involves the uneven development of scrutiny over housing rights. The detailed scrutiny, monitoring and intervention, press campaigns and publicity and the willingness to use Section 23 in respect of the Right to Buy has no parallel in respect of implementation of other housing policy - on meeting need, on homelessness, on providing council housing. Nor has the scrutiny under the Right to Buy been accompanied by examination of the consequences of the Right to Buy or its impact on ability to meet housing need or provide for the homeless. This uneven development of an interventionist philosophy is significant. It is most easily understood if the sale of council houses is seen to be of unusual importance because of its ideological and electoral importance and its role in generating capital receipts. It is also most easily explicable if the political priority relates to a view that there are more votes in the Right to Buy and the expansion of home ownership than in rates of council house building or of provision for the homeless. The most striking contrast between the 1960s and 1980s may then be seen to be in the changing political, electoral and financial assumptions affecting the housing programme.

Increased monitoring and scrutiny inevitably brings central government into unfamiliar territory. It discovers practices of which it does not understand the origin. For example in the Norwich case the refusal to delegate decisions over sale price represents a long established view that direct responsibility for these decisions must rest with elected representatives. The practice did not start with council house sales. Central government does not have the history and experience of local administration which would enable it to deal sensitively with problems of intervention at this level and over-ruling practices which have developed with experience will smack of dictat whether or not they are bad practices.

There is one other perspective on the uneven development of monitoring and scrutiny. This relates to the procedures operated within the central department. One of the most striking features of the Norwich case is the extent to which local decisions, their justification and sequence are open to examination. Some of this is because the case resulted in legal proceedings. But committee and council discussion, press comment on these and publicity given to individual cases involved a degree of public accountability which is not apparent for the central department. There is no equivalent of these enabling scrutiny of the wheres, whys and whens in the Department of the Environment. The Housing Act 1980 granted the Secretary of State enormous discretion and powers of intervention. The processes determining their use and the considerations at crucial stages are not open to scrutiny. All we are aware of is the decision reached and even the documents placed before the court do not provide an account of the considerations made within the central department at crucial stages in the exercise of power.

The lack of accountability of the central department is apparent in more general ways. For example in spite of the recommendations of the House of Commons Environment Select Committee the central department has not regularly reported the decisions it has taken in relation to other discretionary aspects of the Right to Buy (decisions on applications for designated rural area status, decisions on exemption of dwellings as elderly persons' dwellings or on other grounds).

It may reasonably be argued that there is another dimension to this. The local/strategic/landlord ambitions of local authorities could be realised alongside the extension of individual ownership because of the resources released through sales of dwellings. A considerable literature bears on this - on the relationship of receipts from sale to replacement costs, on the level of replacement which would be appropriate in view of reletting rates and on capacity to replace the same with the same and retain or improve the structure of the stock. But there are four additional factors which emerge out of the government's specific policies in this period to frustrate public landlords' capacity to make use of capital receipts: the erosion of levels of loan sanction for housing capital expenditure; the erosion of levels of receipt through discounts; the controls over 'reinvestment' of receipts - only 50% of housing capital receipts could be reinvested between 1980 and 1984, only 40% between March 1984 and March 1985 and only 20% after March 1985; and controls over acquisitions of dwellings by local authorities.

But the significance of the Norwich Saga is not principally about council house sales. As the dispute between central government and the City of Norwich developed the focus of attention was in Norwich's view increasingly on a 'constitutional issue' and on the wording of Section 23 of the Housing Act 1980. The outcome of the court action establishes, in these terms, that Section 23 did rewrite the duties of local authorities and did impose obligations in respect of implementation of certain duties.

The conventional accounts of local authorities' activities commences with the notion of ultra vires - that local authorities are only able to do such things as they can establish a legislative basis for - and moves through a distinction between powers and duties. Local authorities are obliged to carry out duties laid on them by statute - but how they carry them out will vary and is subject to judgements over administration, staffing and costs. Such judgement is subject to legal action but tests of 'reasonableness' apply. It is this kind of test which Norwich felt they could survive. But Section 23 of the Housing Act did not involve a test of this type. Rather, the issue was whether a group of tenants were experiencing difficulty over exercising the Right to Buy. In this way duties under Part 1 of Chapter 1 of the Housing Act 1980 are placed on a different plane from those under other legislation. They are 'priority' duties, their implementation is subject to different types of scrutiny, and performance is accountable in a different way. Section 23 places a duty on the Secretary of State to scrutinise tenants' complaints. The progressive rewriting of duties appears to be opened up by this example. The Housing and Building Control Act 1984 makes some important steps in this direction and the rate-capping measures in the Rates Act 1984 make more substantial steps along the same route - albeit using a different mechanism. In each case the constitutional issue is clear. Central government is placed in a position to decide when and where actions to carry out a range of duties are balanced, correctly prioritised, extravagant or insufficient. The balance of power in determining what is done, following legislation imposing duties, has been shifted significantly towards central government. This shift in power has been part of the conflict between central and local government. In relation to housing over recent years central government has learned and developed the mechanisms for assertion of primacy. Section 23 of the Housing Act 1980 was an 'advance' on the equivalent process in the Housing Finance Act 1972. The wider range of mechanisms and grounds included in the Housing and Building Control Act 1984 mark a further sophistication of measures available to central government.

There is an important distinction which needs to be addressed in this discussion. Much of the literature concerning this area is constructed around local government as the 'problem'. There is a problem variously of efficiency, economy, calibre, political responsibility or radicalism. The problem resides in local government and central government has to cope and respond. But this kind of perspective bears little relation to the Norwich case. Here the new departures, radicalism and push against traditional relationships, came from central government. It is central government that has posed and is the problem. This is even apparent in the style of meetings. Councillors with long experience as members of the ruling party represented continuity and had "learned how to behave". The confrontations were with Ministers enthused by the recent acquisition of office and the zeal of election victory associated with radical new policies. The literature tends to imply that such conflicts involve a reversal of these roles. It is in this context that the question of why Norwich became the frontrunner for intervention is best answered.

Ministers expected some authorities to obstruct. They were determined from the outset to pursue any conflicts. It was this determination on the one hand and Norwich's assessment of the costs and benefits of alternative actions which explains why Norwich faced intervention.

It may be argued that central government can never be the problem. One view of democracy and mandates would not accommodate such a prognosis. It is not intended here to attempt to summarise debates around the superiority or otherwise of different mandates, the subordinate or other status of local administrations compared with central government or the limits of electoral democracy. The existence of a conflicting local mandate obtained on the same day as that referred to by central government, and the existence of conflicting local views of priorities and duties encouraged local stubborn resistance. But in a non-federal system there is no doubt constitutionally and legally about the power of parliament to over-ride any 'local mandate'.

Reasonable judgements? The role of the judiciary

The issue of the role of the judiciary is separate from all of this. Again however there are debates about the independence and neutrality of the judiciary. It is evident that in this case legislation left very limited scope for judicial review. If parliament expresses its intentions clearly enough and legislates for sufficient eventualities the occasions where the courts are left scope to mediate or judge in disputes are very limited. In this case the legislation was sufficiently clear to minimise the scope for review. The judgement delivered in the Appeal Court amounts to a view that the legislation had given the Secretary of State unusual powers. Even the judges sounded surprised to find that parliament had accepted such strong and even draconian powers for a Minister.

Leaving this aside there are aspects of the judicial decisions in this case which raise doubts. The qualifications and experience of judges fell short of what was desirable in some cases. But it can also be argued that some of the comments in giving judgement do not stand up to scrutiny. The judges appear to have accepted the parallel drawn between appeals to the District Valuer on valuations for sales and appeals associated with rating. However, prior to this finding one legal view was that such a comparison was seriously misleading. In the case of a rating decision an appeal to the Local Valuation Court can be followed by a further appeal to the Lands

Tribunal. While the members of Local Valuation Courts are drawn from local valuation panels the Lands Tribunal is a national rather than local valuation court. Members of the Lands Tribunal may be valuers however, raising some of the same issues of professional loyalty. No further appeal applies where Right to Buy valuations are carried out by the DV. The hierarchy and professional relations within the DV's office impose further limits on the adequacy of appeals through this system.

The susceptibility of the Appeal Court judges to the central government view can be illustrated in another way. Although Norwich had frequently referred to the homeless and to households seeking council housing Lord Denning saw the issue as only involving the interests of a trio: central government, the local authority and the council tenant seeking to buy. Where were the homeless or those seeking rented housing? Where were the ratepayers with a financial but not a purchaser interest? Where was the acknowledgement that some council tenants could not make use of the Right to Buy or would have transfer or other opportunities damaged by sales? Lord Denning is not alone in his narrow view of who the issue involved - but it could be expected that he would be more aware of this weakness in the system of administrative justice and the tendency to identify a narrow range of interests.[6]

A last illustration of the very particular perception of housing processes which the judiciary displayed is provided by references made to waiting time. Lord Denning referred to a three month wait for valuation as wholly unacceptable. In one perspective no doubt it is. But in relation to waiting periods for the homeless and those seeking to rent, or for those seeking transfers such a wait is short. In the time scales for the delivery of housing services to individual citizens the period in question is very short. If Lord Denning's perspective is correct then it must be concluded that the failure to provide resources, to carry out monitoring or to use the law in the interests of those who wait longer for housing services tells us something about the interests, priorities and perspectives on duties shared by central government and the judiciary.

It is interesting to note the rather different view of waiting time taken by the Local Ombudsman. In one reported case concerning the Right to Buy an application made in December 1980 was not acknowledged until March 1981 and it was not until August 1982 that papers enabling the sale were sent to the tenant's solicitor. The Local Ombudsman concluded that three months of the delay had been unreasonable and accepted the effects of high workload, properly made policy changes and staffing objectives as excusing delay.[7]

There is a view that the English legal system is particularly ill-equipped to deal with administrative issues such as central-local disputes. The law is geared to protecting the rights of individual citizens. It is in this way that the courts interpreted the Norwich case - in relation to the individuals directly involved in the process. What is demonstrated is the ineffectiveness of the law in dealing with areas of policy where there are conflicts between public agencies. The law is not equipped to act as the arbiter in decisions which are politically defended and does not operate to encourage or open rational debate on public policy issues. The narrow approach of the courts to the interpretation of statutes does not require any appreciation of broader issues in policy decisions and raises doubts about the appropriateness of judicial review to the examination of administrative policies.

Griffith refers to this issue in discussing the 1981 Bromley v GLC case which was concerned with transport policy. He states:

> "The whole method of adjudication as presently adopted by the courts is inappropriate to the consideration of political decisions affecting the distribution of costs between the tax and ratepaying public, on the one hand, and the users of public services, on the other".[8]

Griffith quotes the Comptroller of Finance of the GLC who commented on the judicial process in this case as follows:

> "The process itself was more in the nature of an intellectual marauding over a wide area of hunting territory rather than an ordered, structured, predictable and prepared process. Some issues were dealt with comprehensively and with full intellectual rigour. But others were not and it was not possible to predict on which of many issues a member of the court might concentrate upon at any one time. The basic judicial process of adversarial advocacy, punctuated courteously but irregularly, unpredictably and frequently by important court questions and interjections working from a mound of papers within a necessarily highly concentrated but limited time scale, contrasts sharply with an administrative policy decision which may be an important final expression of

widespread political struggle and practical pressures over a very long period of time".[9]

and Griffith concludes that:

"under their present procedures, judges are ill-equipped to make political decisions which determine the way in which administrative authorities fulfil their duties. The courts of law are not designed as research centres, and judges in our system are most reluctant to assume an inquisitorial role and to seek to discover all the relevant facts. They rely on the adversarial method and take judicial notice only of those matters and those arguments presented to them".[10]

The Norwich case represents a confirmation of these conclusions and can be considered within Griffith's broader analysis of the political function of the judiciary.

Wider perspectives

The academic literature on the state and on central-local government includes a wider range of perspectives. In this section some reference is made to local socialism, bureaucratic dispute, the dual state, the over-extended state, fiscal crisis and legitimation crisis. Some final comments are made on other conflicts occurring in the same period as the Norwich case. In this context it is argued that Norwich is not an isolated case and that discussion of wider perspectives involves a discussion of various developments and cases of which Norwich is only one example.

Local socialism and citizenship rights

The Norwich council house sales saga has been presented previously as a stubborn defence of municipal enterprise and autonomy. It is not an exotic example of vanguard action, the stuff of labour movement legends. There was no mass political action or public demonstration supporting resistance - nor was there mass action expressing discontent with the council. Except for a brief period of campaigning the limited interest in exercising the Right to Buy has remained a feature. The case is not a Poplar or a Clay Cross (and not a GLC). But this is not to diminish the example. It may be argued that Norwich is a more 'representative' example of local socialism than the more exotic cases. The action in Norwich represents the working through of a period of uninterrupted Labour

Party control of a city council; a defence of a situation achieved over a long time period; and a defence couched in the terms of a long established tradition of local control and central-local relations rather than some sudden militancy or left-wing radicalism. Local socialism need not be dramatic and exotic but rests on sustained and determined political activity. There is an argument about whether the Norwich case is more a defence of local control than of socialist objectives. But this would have to take account of the development of collective housing provision, the housing purposes expressed in the case (concerned with relative priorities and notions of need) and the broader priorities of the local authority in developing economic and employment initiatives.

Finally there is an argument that the case is not about localism, socialism or municipalism but about the extension and exercise of citizenship rights. In this perspective the key actions are those of individual citizens exercising their rights. The Right to Buy in this perspective represents a mechanism to redistribute wealth and to shift power from state bureaucracy to the citizen. The Norwich case does involve a group of citizens expressing a demand to share in this process. This was not a mass expression - few complaints and demands were passed to the local authority or local MPs. It is also not clear that it was a 'spontaneous' demand. At least in part it would appear to have been orchestrated and supported by the Conservative Party through various agencies. Nevertheless it is impossible to deny that individual citizens participated in the case. And the involvement was not only in the defence of local government and collective provision.

The dual state

Theories which focus on the interests served by the state cope with disputes between central and local government in different ways. Disputes may be seen as bureaucratic failures rather than fundamental tension or instability. The unitary state which operates at local and national level may experience administrative and communication failures. The Norwich case is rather too prolonged and protracted to be seen in this way. But how does the dispute conform with a model in which central and local state are seen as representing different roles and interests? One model of the dual state which we elaborated in an earlier chapter sees the local state as concerned largely with consumption issues - the delivery of services to individual citizens; and the central state as concerned with investment and accumulation. There are elements of such a division in the Norwich case although in a different form than usually described. The local state was defending its capacity to deliver housing services - but was also asserting its interest in economic and employment issues. More significantly the central state was asserting an interest in the mode of housing consumption for political and ideological reasons but also for fiscal reasons which are consistent with a view of the central state's interest in investment and accumulation. This fiscal interest is returned to later in this section. However these elements of division of interest and areas do not involve functional specificity. The conflict between central and local state reflects the interest of both parts of the state in housing production, consumption and finance. The key to conflict is not some functional specificity or externally determined difference deriving from the nature of the organisations or their statutory basis. The way in which both Norwich and some other authorities and central government responded to a combination of pressures and determinants reflect political choices. The actions taken by Norwich were not taken by all local authorities. Nor were the actions of central government any more 'necessary' or 'inevitable'. The reasons for choosing to proceed with the Norwich case reflect political judgements over the necessary steps to achieve political objectives - not in relation to Norwich alone but in relation to local authorities as a whole. In this respect Norwich was an example used to encourage others rather than the sole or prime offender. While the reasons for central action can be partly expressed in terms of fiscal interest such pressures could have resulted in various actions - with or without the conflict referred to here. The actions of central government were not initially or primarily financial. But the ideological and electoral appeal of council house sales was strengthened progressively by the contribution of capital receipts to public expenditure and monetarist objectives.

The significance of capital receipts from the sale of council dwellings was referred to in Chapter 2. Receipts on this scale are of importance in the whole public expenditure calculus. They are not matters of housing policy and the interest of the Treasury and economic policy considerations are important. Council house sales offered a politically acceptable mechanism of relieving fiscal problems in a period when central government expenditure associated with economic recession was rising in a way that was not desired. The dispute represented in the Norwich case is not the 'familiar' one of local authorities' spending being out of control but of central government spending being out of control and of central government seeking ways of remedying this without raising taxation. A 'raid' on local assets would reduce the borrowing requirements of local authorities and help to achieve monetary and public expenditure policy objectives. In this respect publicly owned housing assets represented an attractive means of achieving fiscal objectives for central government. For local authorities the picture was more complicated. Firstly the dwellings concerned represented a flow of service as well as a realisable asset. Even if full asset values could have been realised the situation would have been complicated. The unique nature of housing assets affects the capacity to replace them through reinvestment - at best it is similar dwellings in similar locations which could be provided. But a second factor highlighted the different positions of local and central government over the issue. Discounts and controls on investment of capital receipts helped central government to achieve its fiscal objectives but introduced an element which would normally be resisted by local authorities - selling at below market value and failing to represent the ratepayers' collective financial interest in the disposal of assets.

Different local authorities have exercised discretion and judgement in these matters in different ways at different times and would no doubt have continued to do so had central government's concern not been enhanced by the uncomplicated and timely fiscal opportunity which selling council houses represented (and the ideological and electoral appeal which it combined).

Rolling back the state?

The Right to Buy has been a major element in pursuing the ideology of individualism and property ownership and a reduction in the role of the state. Ironically, in implementing this policy central government has become more rather than less involved. This has come about in two ways. Firstly the responsibility of central government for specific local patterns of housing tenure and opportunity has been greatly increased. While central government in other areas, notably housing benefits, has sought to identify local administrations with responsibility for service delivery, the opposite has happened in relation to tenure mobility and housing choice. Secondly, and not only in relation to the Norwich case, central government has increasingly become involved in the details of day to day policy implementation. This is apparent not just in taking over council house sales in Norwich but in the extent of monitoring and scrutinising and in the increasing detail of scrutiny. Whereas the Department of Environment had little practical knowledge or experience of issues in conveyancing and restrictive covenants it has become involved in a detailed way and the Housing and Building Control Act provides powers to intervene over this and other areas.

These developments relate to a favourite theme of the New Right: that of the over-extended or overburdened state. This notion derives from two main contentions. First government at central and local level has increased its role to a degree where its failings and lack of competence have become apparent. Second, the libertarian strand of the New Right's critique of the growth of government would point to the intrusiveness of state control and regulation of people's everyday lives. The growth of government has involved increasing failures to deliver what was intended and has been marked by an over-extended bureaucracy which proves inefficient, unresponsive and ineffective. It is argued that the development of local government and of various quasi-non-government organisations is evidence of this. Historically central government has found it more effective to use other organisations than to try to do everything itself. Whether central government uses such agencies (including local government) or becomes more involved in local service delivery and day to day policy implementation (for fiscal or any other reasons) itself the problems of an over-extended bureaucracy become apparent. The Right to Buy represents a response to this situation. It is presented as part of the process of reducing the role of the state and transferring control and ownership to individual citizens. But the Norwich case highlights a contradictory feature. In order to deregulate or demunicipalise services central government has become more rather than less involved in this market. Legislation, publicity, scrutiny and subsidy have all been necessary elements in de-municipalisation. The establishment of a Norwich Office of the Department of the Environment sounds more like a further extension of the state than a disengagement. The questions pursued by that office and the contents of the next legislative step - the Housing and Building Control Act 1984 - involve more and more detail rather than withdrawal. The only logic would be that greater intervention is needed to secure disengagement.

As in other areas of state involvement the consequence, if not the intention, of recent policy development has been to strengthen the central levels of government at the expense of the local levels. Arguably therefore the state is not so much 'rolled back' as withdrawn into a centralist shell less open to democratic demands and public scrutiny. And as central government becomes more obviously directly responsible for local circumstances and living conditions so it becomes the butt for criticism and complaint. It becomes more directly and obviously responsible and is less able to shelter behind other organisations. Thus, in achieving one set of objectives, central government could be diminishing the mechanisms which strengthen and legitimate its role. By changing the established structure of responsibility central government risks upsetting these mechanisms. The increased concentration of power through legislation and other policy action has political implications beyond those of the individual policies themselves. Problems of legitimacy are more likely to arise when the failure to effectively deliver services is unavoidably the responsibility of central government and the failure cannot easily be attributed to other organisations.

Conclusions

This discussion has moved a long way from council house sales and Norwich. It has argued that the Norwich Council house sales saga is really an episode in a process of centralisation which is part of a fiscal and political re-orientation. In order to achieve fiscal and other objectives central government is becoming more involved in local administration. It has introduced legislative measures which have themselves reduced local power and the judiciary have facilitated this centralising tendency. The consequences of this episode for housing and housing policy have been widely discussed elsewhere. Not only do they offer a future of a polarised and segregated housing market with the marginalised poor and the powerless left in the least desirable sectors of council housing, but they offer no solution to problems in the supply and costs of housing. However, in view of the discussion of constitutional and related issues it is appropriate to conclude this study in a different way. What prospects for central and local government are suggested by the Norwich case? Why be a councillor in such an environment? What can local government, ambitious to provide the local services it is mandated to provide, hope to achieve in an environment of centralisation and detailed scrutiny?

The Norwich case terminated with the lifting of the intervention in May 1985. At the same time conflicts around the role and responsibilities of local government and its relationship with central government have become a more common and prominent feature of political debate. Other cases of central-local conflict have different histories and characteristics. And judgements as to what is or is not reasonable will differ. We should be clear, however, of what is shown by the Norwich case and of the precedents and lessons for present and future governments. Central government can change conventions and traditions, and can achieve major changes against the wishes of some local authorities. It can devise legislation which enables it to force stable local authorities with a long tradition of responsible administration, choosing to carry out the law in a 'reasonable' manner, to conform to detailed demands. But at the same time, by becoming more deeply involved in local affairs, it can expose the limits of its own competence, its inconsistencies and can be seen to be pursuing contradictory objectives. In this sense the damage is not limited to local government.

NOTES AND REFERENCES - INTRODUCTION

1. House of Commons, Hansard, 3 December 1981 col 399.

2. G. Jones and J. Stewart, The Case for Local Government (Allen and Unwin, London) 1981.

3. M. Castells, 'Local Government, Urban Crisis and Political Change' in M. Zeitlin (ed) Political Power and Social Theory Volume 2, 1981, p 11 (JAI Press, London).

4. S. Duncan and M. Goodwin, 'The Local State and Restructuring Social Relations', International Journal of Urban and Regional Research Volume 6, 2, 1982, pp 157-185.

5. Castells, op cit, p 4.

NOTES AND REFERENCES - CHAPTER 1

1. See for example L.J. Sharpe (ed), The Local Fiscal Crisis in Western Europe (Sage, London) 1981; N. Fainstein and S. Fainstein (eds), Urban Policy Under Capitalism, Urban Affairs Annual Review, Volume 22 (Sage, London) 1982.

2. J. Gyford, Local Politics in Britain (Croom Helm, London) 2nd edition 1984.

3. See for example discussion in J. Dearlove and P. Saunders, An Introduction to British Politics (Polity Press, Cambridge) 1984, pp 383-384.

4. For a general discussion see M. Boddy and C. Fudge (eds), Local Socialism (Macmillan, London) 1984.

5. C. Cockburn, The Local State (Pluto Press, London) 1977, p 41.

6. P. Dickens and M. Goodwin, Consciousness, Corporatism and the Local State Working Paper No. 26 (Urban and Regional Studies, Sussex University), p 43.

7. See for example S. Duncan and M. Goodwin, 'The Local State and Restructuring Social Relations', International Journal of Urban and Regional Research Volume 6, 2, 1982, pp 157-185.

8. M. Dear, 'A Theory of the Local State' in A.D. Burnett and P.J. Taylor, Political Studies from Spatial Perspectives (John Wiley, London) 1981, p 198.

9. Ibid, p 198.

10. M. Castells, 'Local Government, Urban Crisis and Political Change' in M. Zeitlin (ed), Political Power and Social Theory Volume 2 (JAI Press, London) 1981, p 4.

11. J. Bulpitt, Territory and Power in the United Kingdom (Manchester University Press, Manchester) 1983, p 205.

12. Ibid, p 208.

13. A useful summary of this position is P. Saunders, 'Why Study Central-Local Relations?' <u>Local Government Studies</u> March/April 1982, pp 55-66.

14. P. Dunleavy, <u>Urban Political Analysis</u> (Macmillan, London) 1979; for more recent discussion of these issues see P. Dunleavy, 'The Growth of Sectoral Cleavages and the Stabilization of State Expenditures'. Paper presented to the ISA Conference on Industrial Restructuring, Social Change and the Locality, University of Sussex, 16-19 April 1985.

15. M. Thrasher, 'The Concept of a Central-Local Government Partnership: issues observed by ideas', <u>Policy and Politics</u> 9, 4, 1981, pp 455-470.

16. R. Rhodes, <u>Central-Local Government Relationships</u> Appendix I of SSRC Panel on Central-Local Relations (SSRC) 1979.

17. Saunders 1982, <u>op cit</u>, p 63.

18. These developments are clearly seen in the recent ESRC research initiatives on the Changing Urban and Regional System and Social Change and Economic Life.

19. Duncan and Goodwin, <u>op cit</u>, p 87.

20. Castells, <u>op cit</u>, pp 2-3.

21. J. O'Connor, <u>The Fiscal Crisis of the State</u> (St. James Press, London) 1973.

22. See for example M. Castells, <u>The Urban Question</u> (Arnold, London) 1977.

23. M. Harloe and C. Paris, 'The Decollectivization of Consumption' in I. Szelenyi (ed) <u>Cities in Recession</u> (Sage, London) 1984, pp 70-98.

24. <u>The Government's Expenditure Plans 1985-86 to 1987-88</u> Volume 1, Cmnd 9428 (HMSO, London).

25. For a general discussion see G. Thompson, 'Rolling Back the State? Economic Intervention 1975-82' in G. McLennan, D.

Held and S. Hall (eds), <u>State and Society in Contemporary Britain</u> (Polity Press, Cambridge) 1984, pp 274-298.

26. L.J. Sharpe, 'Is There a Fiscal Crisis in Western European Local Government? A first appraisal' in L.J. Sharpe, <u>op cit</u>, p 7.

NOTES AND REFERENCES - CHAPTER 2

1. A. Murie, The Sale of Council Houses, CURS, University of Birmingham 1975.

2. Conservative Party, A Better Tomorrow, 1970, p 18.

3. Conservative Party, Annual Conference Report, 1971, p 92.

4. Conservative Party Conference, 1972, pp 67-70.

5. Ibid.

6. Ibid.

7. DOE Circular 16 March 1979.

8. Conservative Manifesto, 1979, Conservative Central Office April 1979.

9. Hansard, House of Commons Debates 15 May 1979 cols 79-80.

10. Hansard, House of Commons Debates 15 January 1980 cols 1447-8.

11. Ibid col 1448.

12. Ibid col 1501.

13. Ibid col 1510-11.

14. House of Commons, Parliamentary Debates, Official Report, Standing Committee F, Housing Bill, Eleventh Sitting, 21.2.80 (Morning) col 472.

15. Ibid cols 473.

16. Ibid cols 483-4.

17. Ibid col 489.

18. Ibid cols 490.

19. Ibid col 490-491.

20. Ibid col 491.

21. Ibid col 491.

22. Ibid col 492.

23. Ibid col 495-496.

24. Ibid col 497.

25. Ibid cols 499.

26. House of Commons, Parliamentary Debates, Official Report, Standing Committee F, Housing Bill, Twelfth Sitting 21.2.80 (Afternoon) col 568.

27. House of Commons, Parliamentary Debates, 16.4.80 col 1271.

28. Ibid cols 1293-4.

29. House of Commons, Parliamentary Debates, 20.5.80 col 305.

30. A. Arden, The Housing Act 1980, Sweet and Maxwell 1980 51/23.

31. Ibid.

32. The Guardian 30.5.85.

33. Monica Skinner, Send a commissioner to sell houses says council, Local Government Chronicle 17 October 1980, p1091

34. Stanley will use powers to beat house sales defiance, Municipal Journal 17 October 1980, p 1199.

1. Notes of meeting to consider implications of Housing Bill 15.7.80, p 1.

2. Ibid.

3. Ibid.

4. Ibid, p 2.

5. Minutes of Housing Committee 23.7.80, para 15.

6. Report of Director of Administration and Director of Housing and Estates to Housing Committee 18.8.80.

7. Ibid, para 4.

8. Department of the Environment unpublished statistics.

9. Report of Director of Administration and Director of Housing and Estates 18.8.80, para 5.

10. Minutes of Housing Committee 18.8.80, para 1.

11. Ibid.

12. Report of Director of Housing and Estates to Housing Committee 1.10.80, para 4.

13. Department of the Environment, Audit Inspectorate, Management of Conveyancing in Local Government, HMSO, 1983.

14. Minutes of Housing Committee 7.10.80, p 2.

15. Ibid.

16. Minutes of Housing Committee 19.11.80, para 8.

17. Letter from Director of Housing and Estates to DOE Eastern Regional Office 10.12.80.

18. Ibid.

19. Letter from DOE Eastern Regional Office 28.1.81.

20. Letter from DOE Eastern Regional Office 25.3.81.

21. Letter from Director of Housing and Estates to DOE Eastern Regional Office 29.4.81.

22. Notes of Progress Meeting on Council House Sales 17.2.81.

23. Letter from DOE Eastern Regional Office 23.2.81.

24. File of Complaints Received.

25. Ibid.

26. Minutes of the proceedings of Norwich City Council 3.3.81.

27. Ibid.

28. Eastern Evening News 4.3.81.

29. Eastern Evening News 29.4.81.

30. Ibid.

31. Letter from DOE Eastern Regional Office 1.5.81.

NOTES AND REFERENCES - CHAPTER 4

1. Notes of pre-agenda meeting to discuss items for Mortgages (Joint) Sub-Committee 5.5.81.

2. Ibid.

3. Report of Director of Housing and Estates to Mortgages (Joint) Sub-Committee 13.5.81.

4. Norwich Mercury 1.5.81.

5. Letter to Margaret Thatcher 23.3.81.

6. Letter to Michael Heseltine 22.4.81.

7. Letter to Department of the Environment 6.5.81.

8. Letter to Department of the Environment 28.5.81.

9. Letter to John Stanley 7.5.81.

10. Letter to Michael Heseltine 1.5.81.

11. Letter to Department of the Environment 5.5.81.

12. Letter to Regional Controller (Housing) DOE Eastern Regional Office from Director of Administration 20.5.81.

13. Ibid.

14. Ibid.

15. Letter to DOE Eastern Regional Office 1.6.81.

16. Letter from Regional Controller (Housing) DOE Eastern Regional Office 16.6.81.

17. Ibid.

18. Ibid.

19. Letter to DOE Eastern Regional Office 3.7.81.

20. Ibid.

21. Minutes of meeting of Mortgages (Joint) Sub-Committee 8.7.81.

22. Notes of meeting between officers of Norwich City Council and officers from the Department of the Environment, in London 9.7.81.

23. Ibid.

24. Ibid.

25. Ibid.

26. Ibid.

27. Letter to Chief Executive, Norwich City Council from Under Secretary, DOE Marsham Street 28.7.81.

28. House of Commons, Hansard, 28 July 1981 col 442.

29. Norwich Mercury 8.8.81.

30. From transcript of taped interview.

31. Ibid.

32. Letter from Chief Executive, Norwich City Council to Under Secretary, DOE Marsham Street 13.8.81.

33. Ibid.

34. From transcript of taped interview.

35. Letter from Leader of City Council Norwich to Michael Heseltine, Secretary of State at the DOE 13.8.81.

36. Notes of meeting between representatives of Norwich City Council and those representing the Department of the Environment 15.9.81, para 3.

37. Ibid para 4.

38. Ibid para 7.

39. *Ibid* para 11.

40. *Ibid* para 13.

41. *Ibid* para 17.

42. *Ibid* para 18.

43. Transcript of taped interviews.

44. Eastern Evening News 15.9.81.

45. Minutes of Housing Committee 23.9.81.

46. Letter to John Stanley, Minister for Housing and Construction from Len Stevenson, Leader of Norwich City Council 23.9.81.

47. Norwich Mercury 25.9.81.

48. Letter to Chief Executive, Norwich City Council from DOE Marsham Street 30.9.81.

49. Report of Director of Housing and Estates to Mortgages (Joint) Sub-Committee 14.10.81.

50. Minutes of meeting of Mortgages (Joint) Sub-Committee 14.10.81.

51. Letter from Chief Executive, Norwich City Council to Regional Controller (Housing) DOE Eastern Regional Office 19.10.81.

52. Letter from Michael Heseltine, Secretary of State for the Environment to Len Stevenson, Leader of Norwich City Council 29.10.81.

53. Letter from Len Stevenson to Private Secretary, Secretary of State's Office, Department of the Environment 2.11.81.

54. Transcript of taped interviews.

55. Notes of meeting between representatives of Norwich City Council and the Department of the Environment, Marsham Street, London 5.11.81.

56. Ibid.

57. Ibid.

58. Ibid.

59. Ibid.

60. Ibid.

61. Ibid.

62. Transcript of taped interviews.

63. Letter to the Chief Executive, Norwich City Council from DOE, Marsham Street 6.11.81.

64. Report of Chief Executive to General Purposes Committee, Norwich City Council 10.11.81, para 10.

65. Ibid para 11.

66. Ibid paras 16-19.

67. Ibid paras 20-21.

68. Ibid para 27.

69. Ibid paras 30-32.

70. Ibid paras 39 and 45.

71. Minutes of General Purposes Committee 10.11.81.

72. Letter from Len Stevenson, Leader of Norwich City Council to Michael Heseltine, Secretary of State for the Environment 11.11.81.

73. Report of Housing Manager to Mortgages (Joint) Sub-Committee 9.12.81.

74. Letter to Len Stevenson, Leader of Norwich City Council from Michael Heseltine, Secretary of State for the Environment 3.12.81.

With the exception of the references below all quotations in this chapter derive from transcripts of the judgements delivered in the Divisional Court 18.12.81 and the Court of Appeal 9.2.82.

1. Transcript of taped interviews with officers and members of Norwich City Council 5.12.81 and 7.12.81.

2. Transcript of taped interviews between officers and members of Norwich City Council.

3. M. Loughlin, <u>Local Government, The Law and the Constitution</u> (Local Government Legal Society Trust) 1983, p 62.

1. Report of Chief Executive Officer to General Purposes Committee 10.11.81.

2. House of Commons, Hansard 28.1.82 col 436.

3. House of Commons, Hansard 23.2.82 col 364.

4. New Bid of House Sales 17.2.82, Norwich local press.

5. Ibid.

6. City House Sales Plan approved by Heseltine 22.2.82, ibid.

7. Speeded-up Home Sales mean £5m to City 23.2.82, ibid.

8. Transcript of interview.

9. Some further details of the pattern of sales and purchasers are provided in R. Forrest and A. Murie, Monitoring the Right to Buy 1980-1985, SAUS 1985, forthcoming.

NOTES AND REFERENCES - CHAPTER 7

1. J.A.G. Griffith, <u>Central Departments and Local Authorities,</u> (George Allen and Unwin, London) 1966, p 518.

2. <u>Ibid</u> p 289.

3. <u>Ibid</u> pp 289-90.

4. Evelyn Sharp, <u>The Ministry of Housing and Local Government,</u> (George Allen and Unwin, London) 1969, p 74.

5. J.B. Cullingworth, <u>Housing and Local Government,</u> (George Allen and Unwin, London) 1969.

6. This also relates to the discussion of 'standing' and 'sufficient interest', see C. Harlow and R. Rawlings, <u>Law and Administration</u> (Weidenfeld and Nicolson, London) 1984, pp 299-307, and H.W.R. Wade, <u>Administrative Law</u> (Clarendon Press, Oxford) 1982, pp 619-622.

7. M. Hyde, 'Obstructing the Right to Buy', <u>Housing</u> Volume 21 No. 3, March 1985, p 17.

8. J.A.G. Griffith, <u>The Politics of the Judiciary,</u> (Fontana Press) 1985, p 212.

9. <u>Ibid</u> pp 212-3.

10. <u>Ibid</u> p 220.

APPENDIX A

CHRONOLOGY OF KEY EVENTS

1980

August 8 — Housing Act 1980 received Royal Assent

October 3 — Right to Buy comes into force

1981

February 23 — Norwich receives first letter from DOE concerning tenants' complaints

June 16 — Norwich invited to attend meeting at DOE regarding progress on the Right to Buy

July 9 — Meeting between officers of DOE and Norwich at Marsham Street

July 28 — Statement in House of Commons regarding Norwich and five other authorities
Formal warning that use of Section 23 being contemplated

August 13 — Norwich request meeting with Michael Heseltine

September 15 — Meeting between John Stanley, DOE officers and officers and members of Norwich

September 30 — Letter from DOE conveying Ministers' view that timetable of progress 'totally unacceptable'

October 29 — Michael Heseltine invites Norwich representatives to meeting at Marsham Street

November 5 — Meeting between Heseltine, Stanley, DOE officers and Norwich officers, members and MPs

November 10 — Meeting of General Purposes Committee of council to consider Ministerial demands and council strategy

November 11	Stevenson, Leader of the council writes to Heseltine reaffirming Norwich timetable for issue of formal offers - restates Norwich decision to challenge intervention in court if necessary
December 3	Statement in House of Commons regarding intervention under Section 23 in Norwich
December 4	Notice of intervention received
December 7	Justice Glidewell approves application from Norwich to apply for judicial review and injunction
December 17	Case before Divisional Court
December 18	Lord Justice Donaldson dismisses application
December 21	Application for appeal granted

1982

January 20-27	Case before Lord Denning in Court of Appeal
February 9	Court of Appeal Judgement, Norwich defeated

SECTION 23, THE HOUSING ACT 1980

23.—(1) Where it appears to the Secretary of State that tenants generally, or a tenant or tenants of a particular landlord, or tenants of a description of landlords have or may have difficulty in exercising the right to buy effectively and expeditiously, he may, after giving the landlord or landlords notice in writing of his intention to do so and while the notice is in force, use his powers under the following provisions of this section; and any such notice shall be deemed to be given 72 hours after it has been sent.

(2) Where a notice under subsection (1) above has been given to a landlord or landlords no step taken by the landlord or any of the landlords while the notice is in force or before it was given shall have any effect in relation to the exercise by a secure tenant of the right to buy or the right to a mortgage, except in so far as the notice otherwise provides.

(3) While a notice under subsection (1) above is in force the Secretary of State may do all such things as appear to him necessary or expedient to enable secure tenants of the landlord or landlords to which the notice was given to exercise the right to buy and the right to a mortgage, and he shall not be bound to take the steps which the landlord would have been bound to take under this Chapter.

(4) Where, in consequence of the exercise by a secure tenant of the right to a mortgage a landlord becomes a mortgagee of a dwelling-house whilst a notice under subsection (1) above is in force in relation to the landlord and to the dwelling-house, then, while the notice remains in force—

(*a*) the Secretary of State may, on behalf of the mortgagee, receive any sums due to it and exercise all powers and do all things which the mortgagee could have exercised or done ; and

(*b*) the mortgagee shall not receive any such sum, exercise any such power or do any such thing except with the consent of the Secretary of State, which may be given subject to such conditions as the Secretary of State thinks fit.

(5) Where it appears to the Secretary of State necessary or expedient for the exercise of his powers under this section, he may by notice in writing to a landlord require it within such period as may be specified in the notice or such longer period as he may allow, to produce any document or supply any information ; and any officer of the landlord designated in the notice for that purpose or having custody or control of the document or in a position to give the information shall, without instructions

167

from the landlord, take all reasonable steps to ensure that the notice is complied with.

(6) A notice under subsection (1) above may be withdrawn by a further notice in writing, either completely or in relation to a particular landlord or a particular case or description of case; and the further notice may give such directions as the Secretary of State may think fit for the completion of any transaction begun before the further notice was given.

(7) Directions contained in a notice under subsection (6) above shall be binding on the landlord and may require the taking of steps different from those which the landlord would have been required to take if the Secretary of State's powers under this section had not been used.

(8) Where, in consequence of the exercise of his powers under this section, the Secretary of State receives any sums due to a landlord he may retain them while a notice under subsection (1) above is in force in relation to the landlord, and he shall not be bound to account to the landlord for any interest accruing on any such sums.

(9) Where the Secretary of State exercises his powers under this section with respect to any secure tenants of a landlord he may calculate, in such manner and on such assumptions as he may determine, the costs incurred by him in doing so and certify a sum as representing those costs; and any sum so certified shall be a debt from the landlord to the Secretary of State payable on demand, together with interest at a rate determined by the Secretary of State from the date the sum was certified.

(10) Any sum payable under subsection (9) above may, without prejudice to any other method of recovery, be recovered from the landlord by the withholding of any sum due from the Secretary of State, including any sum payable to the landlord and received by the Secretary of State in consequence of his exercise of his powers under this section.

(11) The references in subsections (5) to (10) above to a landlord and to the powers of the Secretary of State with respect to the secure tenants of a landlord include respectively references to a body which has become a mortgagee in consequence of the exercise by a secure tenant of the right to a mortgage and to the powers of the Secretary of State to act on behalf of such a mortgagee.

HOUSING ACT 1980: SECTION 23
NOTICE OF INTERVENTION BY THE SECRETARY OF STATE
FOR THE ENVIRONMENT

TO: The City Council of Norwich (hereinafter called "the Council"), City Hall, Norwich NR2 INH.

WHEREAS it appears to the Secretary of State for the Environment (hereinafter called "the Secretary of State") that tenants of the Council have or may have difficulty in exercising the right to buy effectively and expeditiously under Chapter 1 of Part I of the Housing Act 1980 (hereinafter called "the Act"):

AND WHEREAS no step taken by the Council while a notice under section 23(1) of the Act is in force or before it was given will, by virtue of section 23(2) of the Act, have any effect in relation to the exercise by a secure tenant of the Council of the right to buy or the right to a mortgage, except in so far as the notice otherwise provides:

NOW THEREFORE the Secretary of State, in exercise of the powers conferred on him by section 23(1) and (2) of the Act and of all other powers enabling him in that behalf, HEREBY NOTIFIES the Council of his intention to use his powers under section 23 of the Act and makes provision as follows:-

1.   Every step taken by the Council before 7th December 1981 (hereinafter called "the relevant date") in relation to the exercise by any secure tenant of the Council of the right to buy or, as the case may be, the right to a mortgage shall have effect.

2.   Where -

   (a)   on the relevant date proceedings are pending between the Council and any tenant of the Council for a determination by a court of any question arising under Chapter 1 of Part I of the Act; or

   (b)   before the relevant date an application in accordance with paragraph 5 of Part I of the Schedule 1 to the Act (hereinafter called "the said paragraph 5") has been

> made by the Council to the Secretary of State for a determination by him under the said paragraph 5,

every step taken by the Council on or after the relevant date in the said proceedings or, as the case may be, on the said application shall have effect.

3. Every application made by the Council in accordance with the said paragraph 5 to the Secretary of State on or after the relevant date in relation to any case where a tenant of the Council served a notice on the Council under section 5(1) of the Act before the relevant date shall have effect and every step taken by the Council on the said application on or after the relevant date shall also have effect.

4. Where before the relevant date pursuant to section 11(2) of the Act a request for a determination or, as the case may be, a re-determination has been made, any representations made by the Council pursuant to section 11(4) of the Act on or after the relevant date shall have effect.

5. Every step taken by the Council on or after the relevant date to which the Secretary of State gives his written consent to the Council shall have effect.

6. The Interpretation Act 1978 shall apply to this Notice as it applies to subordinate legislation made after the commencement of that Act.

3 December 1981   (Signed)
                              Secretary of State

ALSO PUBLISHED BY SAUS

Working Paper 39
Right to Buy? Issues of need, equity and polarisation in the sale of council houses
Ray Forrest and Alan Murie (1984)   £4.65 A4 (118 pp)

A summary of recent research on the impact of council house sales. This report refers to sales prior to the Right to Buy and to the early impact of the Right to Buy. It relates to both academic and policy debates around council house sales and discusses specific issues including the types of dwellings sold, characteristics of purchasers, levels of discount and local variations. The paper concludes with a discussion of sales in the context of broader processes affecting the welfare state in Britain.

Working Paper 40
Monitoring the Right to Buy 1980-82
Ray Forrest and Alan Murie (1984)   £4.25 A4 (85 pp)

This report details progress with council house sales in England under the Right to Buy up to the end of 1982. It refers to national and regional statistics and makes considerable reference to local variations and local case studies. There is also a discussion of financial aspects of the policy which refers to capital receipts, the HRA and the relative costs of renting and buying.

Working Paper 41
A Foot on the Ladder? An examination of low cost home ownership initiatives   £4.90 A4 (150 pp)
Ray Forrest, Stewart Lansley and Alan Murie (1984)

A detailed examination of a range of schemes designed to provide home ownership at low cost, ranging from council house sales to Do It Yourself shared ownership and homesteading. The paper includes a brief historical account of the growth of home ownership, an examination of the contemporary evidence on household preferences and of current government policy, and looks at the scale of provision under the different schemes at a national and regional level, with an analysis of the characteristics of households who have taken advantage of them.

For further details of the above publications and a full list of publications available, please contact the **Publications Officer, School for Advanced Urban Studies, Rodney Lodge, Grange Road, Bristol BS8 4AE.**

All prices include postage.
Cheques should be made payable to the **University of Bristol.**

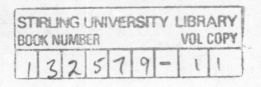